Pay Yourself First

Published by Lynn O. High
First Edition 1984
Second Edition 1985
Third Edition 2017
Fourth Edition 2018

ISBN: 978-1542726511

Table of Contents

Preface

In the first edition of this book published in 1984, my focus was how the average working man and woman could accumulate future wealth; and so it remains in this edition.

If you are already wealthy, good for you! You may have inherited wealth, or you may be one of the "chosen few" who reach great heights as captains of industry, or a movie star or a professional athlete, etc.

If you reach the goal of multiple millions of dollars a year of income, you don't need my book; although all of the concepts apply at any income level.

Realistically, only a few Americans are ever going to see such lofty sums (1-2%); therefore, this book focuses on individuals (and families) who earn income in a range from $25,000 to $250,000.

Based on U.S. Census reports, that includes American families between the twenty-second percentile to the ninety-eighth percentile, or about three-quarters of all Americans.

If you are in that range, and have the desire to accumulate wealth, then regardless of your current income this book is for you.

This revised 2018 edition incorporates the tax law changes passed by congress in

This book continues to focus on three major concepts that remain the same no matter what the tax laws.

The tax code revision passed by congress in December, 2017, has some impact but the three concepts of accumulating wealth still apply. They are truly timeless.

These three concepts are as follows:

1. If you want to create future wealth for yourself and your family, you have to begin by putting aside a portion of your annual income.

2. You have to find a way to reduce income taxes, if possible, on what you put aside.

3. You have to be very good at finding the right types of savings/investment products and assets to create earnings on what you are putting aside. It is this growth in value over your lifetime that will create your future wealth.

IT'S THAT SIMPLE!!!

So what's keeping you from doing it?

Introduction
"Who, What, Where, and Why"

<u>Who am I?</u>

I hope you are a little curious about who I am and what my motives were to write this book.

More importantly where did I find the information I used for writing a work on personal finance? How did I come up with "secrets" and "formulas" for success?

And why would I want to share them with you?

When I published the first edition of this book in 1984 I was an active duty officer in the United States Air Force with 18 years of service. I was not a financial counselor; but I was a financial wizard.

I had been very successful with my personal investments and during an assignment in Honolulu, Hawaii, from 1981-83, I joined a securities firm and became one of its top salesmen.

By that time I had already read extensively about financial practices and attended numerous financial seminars before I wrote the first edition. I will share that history about myself during Part 1.

Today I'm retired from the Air Force and retired from my second career as a special life insurance salesman to community banks all across America. I just retired from a very enjoyable part time position as an advanced income tax preparer where I became an enrolled agent to the IRS allowing me to help many people with IRS audit problems.

By the time I retired from my second career I had clients in twenty-six states and had completed over 400 personal financial plans for the owners and executives of banks.

During the first fifteen years of my second career, when the company I worked for kept count and had an annual "top agent" award, I won it four times.

Believe me that was a huge achievement. We had a group of very competitive salesmen with lots of experience and talent.

For your benefit I now have over forty-five years' of experience with how investments work and, even more importantly, which ones don't.

What has changed?

During the past thirty-four years since I published the first edition of this book, there has been an incredible change in our economy and the investment options for people.

The first factor was the tax reform act of 1986 that drastically lowered the federal income tax brackets. Yes, there really was a 70% tax bracket before that.

Next, traditional pension plans have virtually disappeared in favor of company sponsored 401(k) plans and/or individual retirement accounts (IRA).

Third, interest rates have plunged over the past two decades, and may continue at the current historically low rates for a few more years. But at some point, they will most likely go back up.

Fourth, Social Security has been reformed and improved. Yes, it really has, and I will cover that in the final chapter.

Fifth, and last, life insurance has undergone a complete remake from the traditional "whole life" that your parents or grandparents bought and is now a major part of any sound investment portfolio.

But even with this changing environment, there are still basic bedrock principles from centuries ago that have never changed, and it is these principles ("secrets") that I will share with you and explain exactly how they work.

<u>Where did I learn all of this?</u>

I grew up on a farm in the Midwest where my father had dreams for his children. He made sure that we had the opportunity to go to college.

That was quite an event for young people in the 50's and 60's. I went to college because I wanted to be a pilot in the Air Force and the only way for me to achieve that goal was through the ROTC program offered at major universities.

I had dreamed of being a pilot since I was ten years old. Because my father sent me to college I achieved my dream in September, 1966, when I reported for flying training in Enid, Oklahoma.

I loved to fly and I graduated first in my class. I then spent the next six years flying two different fighter airplanes and serving two years of combat duty in the Vietnam War.

I wrote a book about those experiences in 2015 (which will be identified at the end of this book), but at this moment my focus is on you and how you can achieve your financial goals and dreams for your family and for your retirement.

My first contact with "financial advice" was during my senior year in college. A gentleman who was a former military officer and a member of my fraternity returned to attend graduate school.

One day he dropped by the frat house and was discussing what military service was like and, of course, I listened intently as I was less than a year away from entering the air force.

I hung around for quite a while talking with him about my future. In the course of that conversation he gave me this advice:

"Since you are going to be a pilot, you're going to get an extra hundred dollars a month compared to the other second lieutenants," he said.

Note: base pay back then was $305 a month so that extra hundred was a big deal.

"If you take your flight pay," he continued, "and put it in the bank you will find you can live on your straight base pay the same as the other new officers. Then, if you do that your whole career, you will be pleasantly surprised at how much money you will have saved by the time you retire."

Did I do that?

Of course not!

When I arrived at pilot training I quickly found an extra hundred dollars a month allowed me to buy a new car and spend a lot of time and money on dating young ladies.

Sometimes I wonder how I ever had the time to study and graduate first in my class.

<u>Why am I sharing my experiences with you?</u>

Do not misunderstand me. I know people generally write a book for three reasons:

First, the notoriety of being a published author -- it sounds good at cocktail parties;

Second, altruism -- feeling good about helping others; and

Third, money -- they (as I) hope it will be a best seller.

Yes, I will earn a small royalty for your having bought this book; but please note that I have no seminars, no proprietary software systems, nor anything else to sell you.

I am not a "get rich quick scheme seminar promoter." I have been to many of those and tried a few.

So don't fall for those radio ads urging you to flip houses or buy some software to pick the winners in the stock market. Ninety-five percent of people who do so only make the promoter rich.

My primary purpose is to share what I have learned over the past forty-five years with you and all you will ever pay me is my author's royalty for buying this book.

In the final section of this book on what worked for me, and what didn't, I will share why that is so important.

I have updated this book to reflect my experiences with a host of different investments; and the major changes in the income tax code that have occurred since 1986 (2018 being the current major change).

This book is a compendium of my experiences and is based on a universal truth stated most eloquently in a ninety year old book titled "The Richest Man in Babylon." In that book the author shares this simply truth: "A part of all you earn is yours to keep."

From that comes this book's title: "Pay Yourself First."

9

But the real truth is simply this -- unless you are going to inherit great wealth, or marry the banker's daughter or son, or invent that one in a million product that nearly all of mankind will buy (think Facebook, Microsoft, Polaroid, Henry Ford (auto), Rockefeller (oil), Carnegie (steel), Ray Kroc (McDonalds) etc.), then the only way for you to accumulate any degree of wealth in the future is to do it the old fashioned way -- EARN IT!

That is the real truth for three quarters of all Americans.

This book will inspire you to follow a systemic method of keeping a part of all you earn and show you a basic investment strategy to reach your financial goals.

With that in mind grab your highlighter and let's get going.

Part 1
"The First Secret"

The single greatest asset the vast majority of us will ever have in our lifetime is our individual earning power from our chosen profession, talent, or skill.

In 2012, the generally accepted average for a college graduate's potential lifetime earnings was $2,300,000; for a doctoral degree it increased to $3,200,000; for a high-school graduate it was around $1,400,000.

NOTE: These values are in present day dollars based on a forty year working career and discounted at three percent. In that way these sums can be compared to present day salaries and living expenses (total purchasing power).

But the actual potential for a college graduate in actual dollars based on the average starting salary in 2015 of $45,478, and an annual average increase over time of three percent (3.0%), is a total of $3,400,000 over forty years.

That is what you will actually have to work with -- or possibly more based on your position and success.

Whatever your position your lifetime earning power is a lot of money. The question is, "How much will you have kept by the time you retire?"

In spite of this tremendous earning power, 80 to 85% of Americans reach age 65 and don't have any real wealth to show for it. They will spend their retirement years not in dignity but at a lower standard of living than they enjoyed in the prime of their working years.

For those who have children, poor financial management may deny those children the opportunity to achieve more for themselves than their parents commonly called "the American Dream."

Why? Because their parents simply didn't know how to financially plan for them.

You see, the majority of Americans were not brought up or trained to be financial geniuses; as a result, most Americans are financial illiterates.

It's not their fault they weren't trained in finance. Doing so is not a requirement for most schools of higher learning or skilled training programs.

As a result there is no one to blame until it is too late. Then most people just blame it on bad luck or the government or they worked for the wrong company that didn't have enough benefits.

There are hundreds of excuses for not doing something, but the cause is simple -- procrastination and the lack of knowledge

As a result you let your lifetime earning power slip through your fingers just like sand.

But that can be changed if you want.

By the end of this Part 1 you will learn how to use the first of three secrets. It is a simple secret but a very effective one.

Chapter 1: "The Richest Man in Babylon"

The Richest Man in Babylon is a book by George Samuel Clason which dispensed financial advice through a collection of parables set in ancient Babylon.

Originally a series of separate informational pamphlets distributed by banks and insurance companies, the pamphlets were bound together and published in book form in 1926.

Through individual character's experiences contained in the parables, the characters learn simple lessons in financial wisdom in managing business and household finance.

As an example, in the second story of that book, Arkad, now the richest man in Babylon, relates his wisdom to a group of boyhood friends who have come to him to ask how he has so much while they have so little.

Arkad tells of how he met Algamish, a wealthy money lender, who simply advised him that by saving a tenth of his income for a year he would have enough to invest in a way to earn more. The most important thing Algamish told him was:

"A PART OF ALL YOU EARN IS YOURS TO KEEP."

For the next year Arkad did as he was told and then invested that money with a brick maker who went on a journey to buy jewels for Arkad to trade.

Upon the brick maker's return the jewels turned out to be worthless pieces of pretty glass. The brick maker had been cheated.

Arkad related this to Algamish, and Algamish castigated Arkad for this foolishness saying, "Every fool must learn. Why trust the knowledge of a brick maker about jewels? Would you go to the bread maker to inquire about the stars?"

Algamish then said to Arkad, "He who takes advice about his savings from one who is inexperienced in such matters will pay with his savings for proving the falsity of their opinions."

Arkad then saved his money for another year but this time he invested it with Agger the shield maker who used it to buy materials for his work. Every fourth month Agger paid Arkad rent for the use of these funds.

Arkad then spent these dividends he received from Aggar on fine clothing and regularly scheduled feasts.

Once again, Algamish castigates Arkad for "eating the children of his savings" by not investing them.

Arkad leaves Algamish and determines to adjust his behavior. He will follow Algamish's advice exactly as he was told.

Two years pass and Arkad again meets with Algamesh, but this time he has a growing fund of coppers to show. Algamish is so pleased with how Arkad has taken his lessons to heart that he hires Arkad as a manager of his estate in Nippur.

By continuing to save and invest wisely, Arkad relates to his friends that this was how he became the wealthy man he is now.

This story was the inspiration of my original book. It all began in 1973 when I was stationed at Williams Air Force Base near Phoenix, Arizona. I had just returned from my second combat tour in Vietnam and was flying F-5 "Freedom Fighters."

One day after a mission I was sitting in the pilot's lounge where one of the older pilots in the squadron was talking about a seminar he had attended a week before. He told how he heard the story about the richest man in Babylon from centuries ago and how the principles of gaining wealth back then still worked today.

He really got my attention.

I asked about going to the seminar and he gave me a phone number to contact the host. I called the next day and talked to the investment salesman who sponsored the seminar and promptly made a reservation to attend the next one in two weeks.

The seminar was fascinating. I heard the same story I just shared with you from the book, "The Richest Man in Babylon," and I immediately took the concept of saving ten percent of my income to heart. After all I was single and a captain on flight pay status.

And then it hit me. This new concept that I embraced was nearly the same idea that had been shared with me while in college seven years before (I mentioned that in the Introduction).

Just like Arkad I too had wasted my time and energy on fine clothing and food. And now I was twenty-nine years old and just as broke as Arkad. I had allowed seven years to pass and I would now have to make up for it!

I left that seminar and vowed to start immediately.

The next day I called the host salesman and arranged to begin an allotment of ten percent from my monthly pay into a mutual fund that had been presented at the seminar. I had to start someplace and this was as good as any.

I also began to read all I could about investments and taxes. Although I had a degree in economics and had studied basic finance, I quickly learned I was not well informed.

I enrolled in a night course at Arizona State University on taxation followed by an accounting course. And that is how I began my journey that lead to the first edition of this book in 1984.

But along the way to doing that I had two big events occur before I published that first edition.

The first event was attending a "Nothing Down" seminar in Las Vegas, Nevada, in 1979 (I was now stationed at Nellis AFB).

The seminar's concept was to buy single family houses and then turn them into rentals. These seminars were all in vogue in California and had spread to Nevada.

At that time mortgage laws were very lax on assumptions, and under President Carter double digit inflation was occurring; thus, the single family home market was blazing. Mortgage interest rates were going up every month.

I had just bought my personal residence using my VA loan to pay one hundred percent of the cost. I was lucky as I locked it in at ten percent interest as it went up to eleven percent the next week, and eventually hit twelve percent after that.

Does this sound at all like what our country just went through during the great recession of 2007-2009?

From what I learned at the seminar I quickly ended up owning seven rental houses in Las Vegas, all with less than five percent down. (Note: I did not buy the seminar course to get to Nothing Down.)

The concept was to assume the first mortgage (an FHA or VA loan) and get the homeowner to give a second mortgage for their equity balance. These second mortgages were usually at ten to twelve percent interest only with a balloon payment in five years.

Why was this possible? Because Las Vegas had an annual turnover of about 30-40% of inhabitants at that time so the supply of houses for sale exceeded the buyers.

Most of these houses were in the lower cost range and would rent for more than the first mortgage payment. And under President Reagan's 1981 tax reform act I could write off all of the paper losses against my salary. It was tax advantaged money for the taking.

The second big event that occurred for me was in late 1981. I had been transferred to Honolulu, Hawaii, in September and once again a friend invited me to an investment seminar a couple of months later.

At this time limited partnerships in real estate, oil and gas, cable TV and commodities had hit the market place as the tax advantaged deals *de jour.*

But this seminar also offered something else. If you wanted to pay for a training course and an SEC acceptance fee you could obtain a securities license and become a "finder" for the company.

If you passed the SEC exams you became a registered representative and were then allowed to bring prospects to the seminars. If they bought any of the offerings you would receive a small commission.

I jumped on it. After quickly passing the two required securities exams (I had gained an MBA a year before), the next step was to make cold calls to lists of doctors and other wealthy prospects.

What an experience that was!

Talk about stuttering. I was a lieutenant colonel who had faced anti-aircraft fire, surface to air missiles and enemy fighters in the Vietnam War, but calling a total stranger and getting him or her to come to a seminar was living hell for me.

But I preserved and after a couple of sales I earned the right to become an independent salesman (which paid even more).

What I learned from this company flabbergasted me. I had no idea how the U.S. Tax Code was so full of loopholes and benefits for those who had the money to use them.

With the federal income tax rate at fifty-percent in 1981, and state income tax rates at three to eight percent, selling tax shelters to upper income people was like selling ice in hell.

I quickly became a master salesman and in the next five years was this company's top salesman two times; and the company had over 200 sales representatives.

From Hawaii I was sent to Montgomery, Alabama, to the Air War College for ten months in 1983 and that is where I wrote the first edition of this book.

I now had stock investments, real estate, oil wells, and commodities. I was riding high.

"Algemish" would have been proud of his new "Arkad."

Chapter 2: Poverty Consciousness

What is poverty consciousness? And why am I writing about this topic at the beginning of this book -- a book on how to gain wealth.

You want to learn the three secrets you were promised, right? But before you can use those three secrets you must attain a state of mind to accept them and implement them.

You must believe you are worthy of having them and using them to achieve what you most likely considered to be impossible – becoming wealthy.

How do I know this? Because you bought this book!

It is not easy to acquire wealth; it is hard to do. It requires you to make a mental commitment to change your beliefs about money, and about what is important to you in life.

Only then will you be able to fulfill the financial goals you set for yourself and your family.

Love of Money

In the first edition of this book the chapter that discussed this need for change in your mental state was titled Love of Money.

However, since I wrote that over three decades ago, I have revised my thinking to more accurately describe this state of mind as poverty consciousness.

Let me set the stage right up front.

In the New Testament of the Bible, Jesus tells us that it is harder for a rich man to enter the kingdom of heaven than for a camel to pass through the eye of a needle.

And we have all been told that love of money is the root of all evil. (Actually some say the lack of money is the root of evil.)

In other words, as we grew from childhood to adulthood, every one of us, including nearly every human being on the planet, has been socialized to accept that great riches are not for us (meaning you or me).

Conversely, we have also been told little truisms like:

"Save for a rainy day."

"Waste not, want not."

"A penny saved is a penny earned."

From this and other studies I have made in the past thirty years I have revised my thinking to be the following.

We have been led to believe that we cannot be rich. We cannot achieve great wealth. That is reserved for the few, the Rockefellers, the Hiltons, and the Gates. Or the few that become super stars of the entertainment world or athletes that climb the ladder to the top of their individual game.

I consider that way of thinking to be poverty consciousness. But let me spring it on you another way.

What is happiness? Are *you* happy? Do *you* pursue the personal goal of being happy? And if you do what are the things or people that make you happy?

In fact, our state of happiness and our state of poverty/wealth are both tied to the same barometer. Our mind!

Psychologists tell us that the human mind is always in a state of consciousness of either happiness or unhappiness; as well as either a state of wealth or poverty.

In other words, YOU decide if you are happy or wealthy. Not someone else. Not your possessions or your bank account, but YOU.

I confirm this to you today as a person of seventy plus years of life because I have been on both sides of both of these equations at some time in my life.

And the most incredible thing is that I have been happy when I had little; and unhappy when I had been given much.

I have been poor with a seven figure income; and rich on a second lieutenant's pay.

Why?

Because it is what I did with each and every situation I was in. Before I became a second lieutenant, for the four prior years, I washed dishes while in college and worked on the family farm in the summer. Neither one a great paying situation; but, they were happy times as I was on a quest to gain my gold lieutenant's bar and begin my new life.

When I graduated college and entered the air force I suddenly had a guaranteed monthly income and a new position of esteem. My life was incredibly good. I literally had more money than I could spend (remember the story of an extra hundred a month for being a pilot I shared earlier).

I was happy and I felt I was rich.

I bought a new car, had a beautiful new girlfriend, and was on my way to become a jet pilot and see the world -- my boyhood dream.

Poverty Consciousness

Simply put, every human being is in a state of wealth or poverty in their mind each and every day.

I base this on having seen people in total poverty in many parts of the world, some of whom do not know what they will have to eat the next day, but they are happy.

Why? Because they have not fallen into the trap of greed or allowing material things to define them. They can love, laugh and enjoy each day to the fullest based on whatever they have.

Conversely, there are the rich and famous people that kill themselves with drugs or alcohol at young ages when, in my view, they had everything one could possibly dream of at their beck and call.

Yet they were so unhappy that they lived in a state of angst and eventually killed themselves, either slowly or by suicide.

Why? Because many humans cannot accept great wealth; either they believe they do not deserve it or they simply cannot handle it. Either way they are unhappy and die in a state of mental poverty -- even with millions in the bank.

Your Choice

Before you read the remainder of this book, you must ask yourself three questions.

Are you happy? Is today a delight for you to be alive?

Are you rich or are you poor? Only one can be your mindset.

Do you want to acquire future financial wealth? If so what is your plan to do that?

Final Thought

There are two great movies that I suggest you see, and even if you have seen them before find them and watch each one again.

They are: "The Bucket List" released in 2007 with two incredibly talented super stars, Jack Nicholson and Morgan Freeman; and "Groundhog Day" released in 1993 with Bill Murray.

I say this because both of these movies had an impact on my life. Groundhog Day contains more subtle and direct examples of what is important in life than any other movie I have ever seen (and I have seen over a thousand movies).

It does it through irony and paradoxical situations. You may need to watch it several times in order to find all of the hidden meanings contained in this film (I had to).

The Bucket List contains more about what brings happiness in life than many similar movies that have come before it (I think of A Christmas Carol or The Gift of the Magi).

It made me realize that every day is a special gift, a gift that I refuse to squander for I don't have that many left due to both my age and having recently faced the big "C" word.

Once you really spend time seeing these two movies I think you will better understand this book and the three secrets that will show you how, on an average income, you can become wealthy beyond your dreams.

Why? Because poverty consciousness will no longer hold you back. You will define wealth on your own terms, and, perhaps as a by-product, find happiness by being able to create your own personal path for attaining both.

I guarantee it.

"Money is the seed of money, and the first guinea* is sometimes more difficult to acquire than the second million."

- Jean Jacque Rousseau (1712 – 1778)

*A gold coin minted in Great Britain from 1663 to 1814 worth 1.1 Pound Sterling (21 shillings).

Chapter 3: "Pay Yourself First"

The first secret of gaining wealth for the average person is obviously: "Pay Yourself First."

I didn't invent it. No, I learned it in February, 1973, when that older gentleman in my flying unit I described in Chapter 1 invited me to attend a financial planning seminar.

I went to that seminar not intending to buy anything but what I learned that night became the basis for my future financial success.

But the most astounding part of the concept outlined that night was essentially the same advice I had been given seven years earlier before I graduated from college (I mentioned this in the Introduction).

In Chapter 1 I gave you a story that was presented that February night evolved around the story of a young man sitting on a street in ancient Babylon.

I want to refresh that story with another episode of possible dialogue that may have occurred between the rich man and another young man. Let's listen to that conversation.

When the young man got up the nerve to ask the rich man how he became so wealthy, the rich man's reply was a question.

"Young man, do you give of your income to your god at your temple?"

The young man replied that he did and in the custom of tithing (ten percent of what he was paid).

The rich man then asked, "And what do you do with the other ninety percent?"

The young man replied that he used it to live on.

The rich man then said, "If you can live on ninety percent you can also live on eighty percent. As you do with your god pay unto thyself in the same manner."

The young man was so taken by this information that he immediately began to set aside ten percent of what he was paid and after a few months he had a bag of copper coins.

Soon he saw the rich man walking down the street again so he approached him and said, "I have been paying myself first, so what shall I do with the money I have accumulated?

The rich man answered, "Put your money to work in something that will earn a profit. Then, when you have accumulated more, do it again. But never stop paying yourself first."

The young man thought about these words and remembered that he had an uncle who traveled with the great caravans to the distance reaches of the world. He could trust his uncle with his bag of coppers. So he went to his uncle and asked him to buy a rug for him on his next trip.

Upon his uncle's return the young man set out into the streets after his day's work and tried to sell his rug. He soon learned that selling was quite a task; it was not easy; but in time he prevailed.

Upon selling the rug he had a small number of silver coins to show for his labor. He was very happy.

In the meantime he had also been saving his coppers from his daily work so he took his bag of coppers plus his new silver coins back to his uncle and asked him to buy three rugs on his next trip.

And soon, after repeating it time and time again, the young man no longer worked for coppers but had the largest rug shop in Babylon.

And one day, years later, a young man stopped him in the street to ask how he had become so rich.

Every journey starts with the first step

I was not a young man in Babylon, but that story I heard at the seminar I attended hit me hard.

I have previously related that in January, 1973, I was twenty-nine years old, had just returned from my second combat tour in the Vietnam War where I had literally spent all my money on booze, food, my Thai lady friend, travel and other adventures.

With the threat of death hanging over me every time I flew it was easy to lead a profligate life in Thailand.

Although I didn't have a "copper" to my name when I came back to the states, I did have a good income that far exceeded my expenses.

So after attending the seminar I made a resolution -- I would pay myself first.

My first step was to establish an account with a mutual fund from the sponsor of that seminar. I then set up what was known as an allotment from my military paycheck for ten percent of my gross pay to be sent every month to that mutual fund.

I soon realized that I still had extra money, but having the deduction from my paycheck was unwieldy. It took a trip to the finance office to change and two months to become effective.

To better manage my investment money I decided to set up a new bank account where I could have the allotment sent, as well as have the profits from my stock investments deposited back into that same bank account.

I then continued with this investment strategy over the next seven years. That is all I did; stock mutual funds. And as they went up and down, I was always buying them at both the low points as well as high points (this is known as dollar cost averaging).

27

But the important part was I was consistent as over the next seven years as I was transferred four times. Stability was not a part of a military career, nor of many others (possibly yours).

But my paycheck allotment was always made and that bank account still exists to this day (it now receives my military retirement check and the money still flows to investment products).

I further made the resolution that as I received additional pay raises, such as annual cost-of-living adjustments, longevity raises, or promotions to a higher rank, I would take half of each raise and increase my allotment to my bank account by that amount.

Accumulation account

It's really important that you have the method of paying yourself first separated from your daily life expenses. That is why setting up a separate bank account is so important.

If you try and use your existing checking account(s), you will most likely fail to stay the course. From time to time your living expenses may overrun your income and you will stop paying yourself first. By having a separate deposit go into your accumulation account you will always be building your wealth for the future.

(See the chart of an Accumulation Account on the next page.)

In today's world, if you are married, most likely your spouse also works. Managing your combined incomes may be a source of occasional conflict.

Please don't have a joint checking account that both of you draw from; you will bounce checks by not keeping track with each other and perhaps argue over who did what. Division of money works much better.

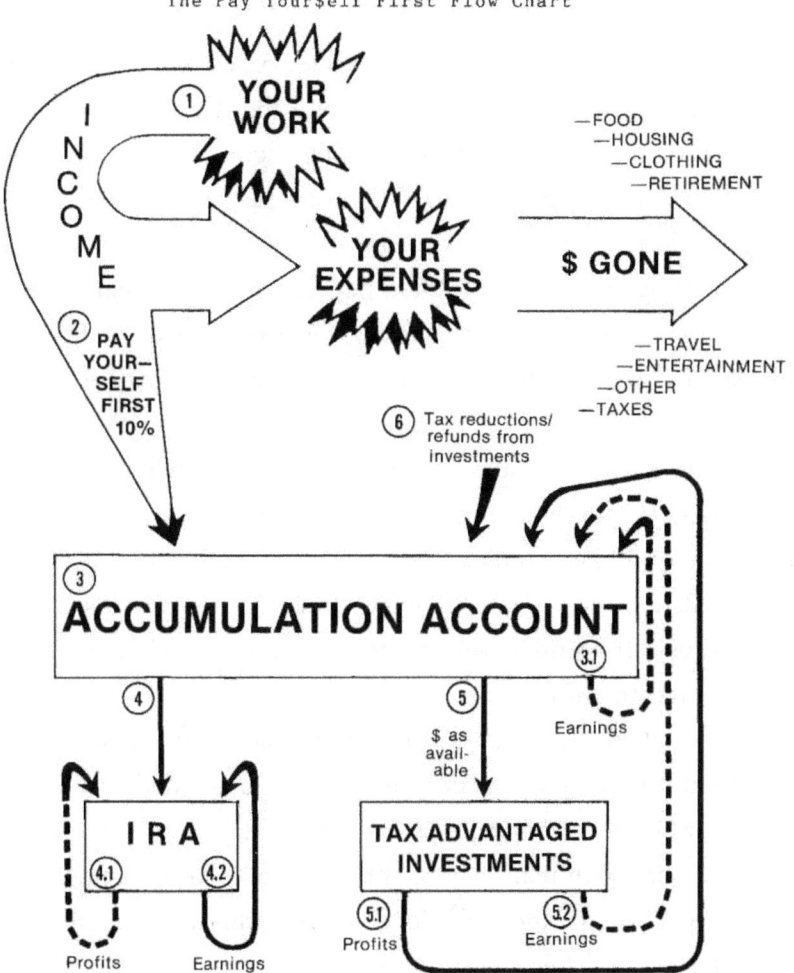

NOTE: I also learned that having special savings accounts for specific purposes like "vacation" or "new furniture" are important. It keeps you (and your spouse) on point about where your paychecks are going.

The simple fact is no matter whether you are 25, 35, 45 or 55, reading this book can make paying yourself first work. Here is how you do it.

Go to your employer and elect to have some percent of your pay sent directly to a separate checking account that I call the Accumulation Account. This is a checking account with no paper checks as you are never going to use it for your ordinary expenses -- those are paid from your other account(s).

Even if you can't do the full ten percent right away start with something -- even one percent. And if you are married and both work each of you does this. You must both be committed to your financial future.

If for some reason your employer won't give you a second separate deposit into your accumulation account then set up a "bill pay" withdrawal from your regular checking account to do it automatically on the same day you get paid. Do not spend it first.

You must differentiate this money no matter what. It is your sole source of investment funds.

NOTE: Later I will discuss your 401(k) plan contributions in the third secret as it is normally an automatic deduction by your employer before you even get paid.

Once your accumulation account is funded and operating you then set up automatic monthly deposits from this accumulation account into your other investments.

Diversification will be addressed later in the third secret, but suffice it to say for today, at this moment, you will at least have three to five other investments to fund and your accumulation account will be the source for all of that funding.

Now, once more, let me repeat.

1. It is really important to have your investment funds segregated from your living expense accounts.
2. Both spouses must be practicing Pay Yourself First.
3. Manage your investment money together.

Remember, it is your money – it's what you do with it that counts.

Income Analysis

Let's begin with some analysis of your income and your paycheck.

DISCLAIMER: The figures you will be reading are mine. They are based on my own compilations from an array of data from open sources such as the Bureau of Labor Statistics, The Census Bureau, et al.

It is important that you understand that statistics are never exactly going to be like you. These are averages of millions of people.

As such it is impossible, without sitting down with you and using what you have as income, to even begin to get an accurate analysis.

What I am presenting here will simply allow you to apply the concepts and principles you will learn in this book to your situation.

Having said this let's begin.

Who are "you"

The census bureau tells us that the average household in the U.S. has 2.3 people. Good luck to that 0.3 person.

Averages never tell the true story. Obviously, if you are single you are a household of 1.0. If married with no children 2.0, and if you have children it is pretty hard to have a 0.3 child, although my mother once said I had only half a brain after I had done something stupid!

The only value of statistics is they can steer you to find out more about yourself (or family) and allow you to compare yourself (or family) to others.

"Where do I stand?" is not an uncommon question everyone asks about their own situation.

The census bureau tells us that in 2016 the median household income was $59,039 (up from $53,657 in 2014 and $57,230 in 2015). In real dollars these are about seven percent lower than the peak household incomes recorded in 1999. (Note: all income amounts are provided based on a baseline for inflation, thus they are "real" only in the year reported.)

The chart on the next page is the distribution of household income in the U.S. for 2011.

NOTE: Census data is only provided every five years and the 2016 chart has not yet been published. If you can remember what you made in 2011 (look at a tax return) this will suffice.

You may be startled at "where you stand" on this chart -- but you cannot begin a journey if you don't know where you are before you start. Over time nearly every household will move upward in gross income due to promotions, cost of living raises, or a job switch.

Distribution of annual household income in the United States
(2011)

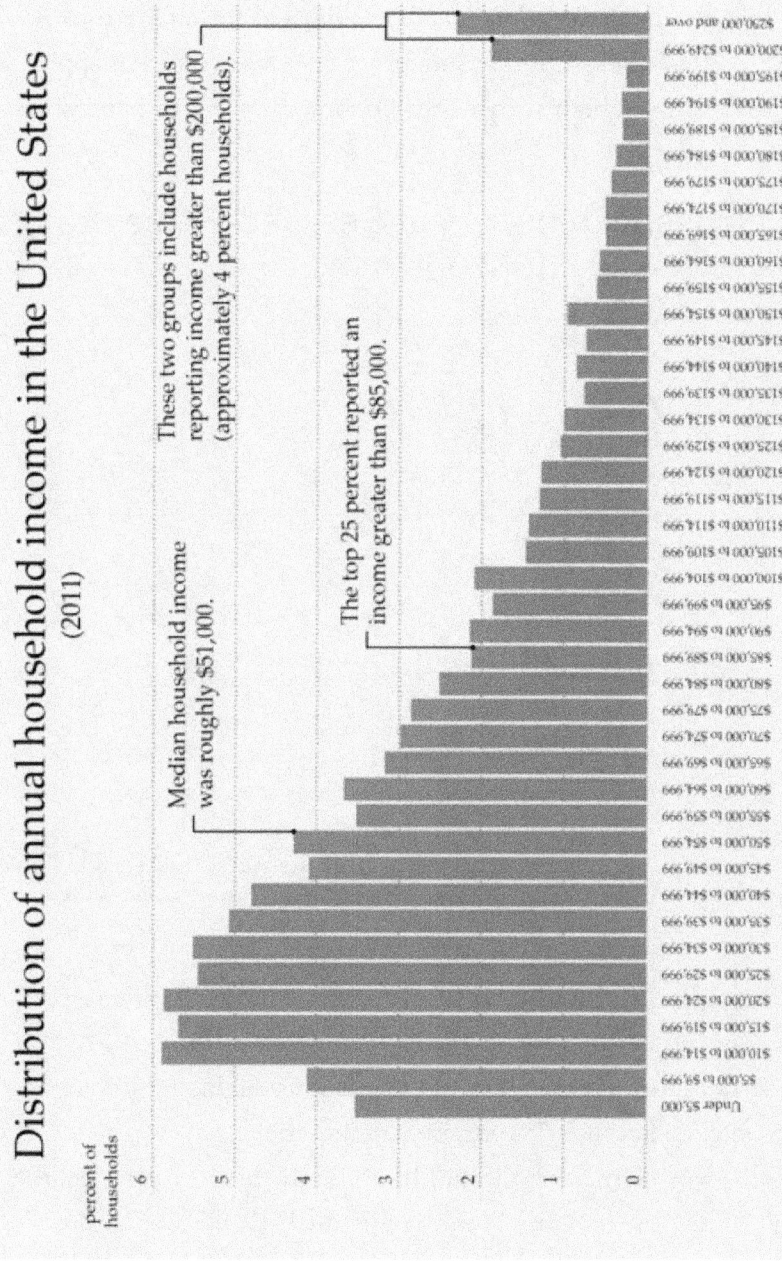

percent of households

Median household income was roughly $51,000.

These two groups include households reporting income greater than $200,000 (approximately 4 percent households).

The top 25 percent reported an income greater than $85,000.

Source: U.S. Census Bureau, Current Population Survey, 2012 Annual Social and Economic Supplement

This next chart is in real dollars based on 2014 as the base. That means that all prior year's data has been adjusted for inflation to convert to 2014 dollars (purchasing power) so that you have apples to apples. It shows the history of real income by selected percentiles.

Real Household Income at Selected Percentiles: 1967 to 2014

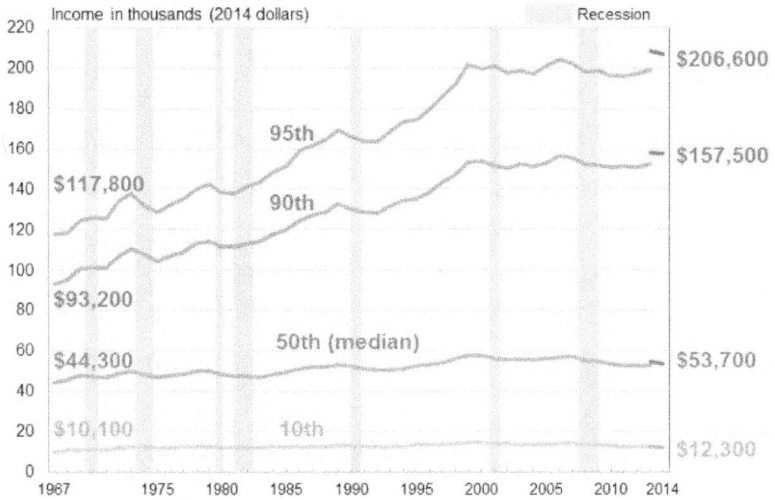

Note: The 2013 data reflect the implementation of the redesigned income questions. See Appendix D of the P60 report, "Income and Poverty in the United States: 2014," for more information. Income rounded to nearest $100.
Source: U.S. Census Bureau, Current Population Survey, 1968 to 2015 Annual Social and Economic Supplements.

The single most interesting thing on this chart is that there had been a slow but steady growth in real income from 1967 to 1999. Then, in 1999, real income became stagnant at the higher percentiles and actually fell about 5-7% for median income.

That is why so many households across the board today feel the "pinch" of income to support their individual standard of living.

34

As I write this revised edition in early 2018 it appears that inflation has been flat until late 2017 and real incomes may be on the verge of rising somewhat.

The stock market has been soaring; however, housing costs have also been rising at a significant rate beginning in 2015 as well as housing rents. So for many people any gain in real income has been used to simply pay for higher costs of housing.

The goal of your reading this book is that by paying yourself first you will be able to sustain your income level for life, send your children to college, own a retirement home, and be able to do the things you want as you go through your working years and into retirement.

If I can inspire you to do that I have earned the price you paid for this book.

Your Paycheck

Have you ever wondered where it all went at the end of the month? I did.

And although I never really did a budget I did keep track of most of my expenses via credit card statements and by keeping tax records each year. But overall I have always been surprised at the number of people that have no idea where their money goes.

To find out what the average person spends, the following chart on the next page will allow you to compare yourself to other households.

Let's take look.

CATEGORY	YOUR ANNUAL INCOME							
	$ 25,000		$ 50,000		$ 75,000		$ 100,000	
FEDERAL INCOME TAX	642	2.57%	3,530	7.06%	6,623	8.83%	8,462	8.46%
SOCIAL SECURITY TAX	1,913	7.65%	3,825	7.65%	5,738	7.65%	7,650	7.65%
HOUSING	8,560	34.24%	15,130	30.26%	20,693	27.59%	26,100	26.10%
TRANSPORTATION	3,567	14.27%	7,666	15.33%	11,227	14.97%	13,629	13.63%
FOOD	3,353	13.41%	5,648	11.30%	8,255	11.01%	9,799	9.80%
PERSONAL INSURANCE/RETIREMENT	1,213	4.85%	3,530	7.06%	7,044	9.39%	13,362	13.36%
HEALTH	1,855	7.42%	3,328	6.66%	4,403	5.87%	4,454	4.45%
ENTERTAINMENT	1,141	4.57%	2,118	4.24%	3,412	4.55%	4,454	4.45%
APPAREL	785	3.14%	1,513	3.03%	2,201	2.94%	2,940	2.94%
CASH PAYMENTS TO OTHERS	642	2.57%	1,311	2.62%	2,091	2.79%	3,385	3.38%
ALCOHOL AND TOBACCO	428	1.71%	706	1.41%	991	1.32%	1,158	1.16%
EDUCATION	357	1.43%	555	1.11%	881	1.17%	1,069	1.07%
PERSONAL CARE	285	1.14%	555	1.11%	826	1.10%	2,316	2.32%
MISCELLANEOUS	428	1.71%	706	1.41%	1,101	1.47%	1,514	1.51%

36

As you find yourself on that chart consider these additional data points from the BLS:

> 1. The average household spends about $6,700 on food: $3,900 on food at home; and $2,600 eating out!

> 2. The average family should spend no more than ten percent on non-mortgage debt. What is your car payment? Student loans? Other personal loans?

> 3. The average lower income family spends $200 on bank overdraft fees; and low income families even more.

The point of the above is simple -- are you wasting money on things that you have allowed to happen out of your control or don't need?

The reason why a budget analysis is so important is that if you are at an income level that requires you to spend it all every month, then you cannot pay yourself first.

For many of you reading this you are going to have to find where you will get the money to pay yourself first. Many a current household is totally committed to spending their full income.

If that applies to you then you have two choices. Keep spending it all and reach retirement (as nearly 85% of Americans do) and have less money to live on than when you worked; or...

...find where you can reduce your spending and begin paying yourself first.

Hopefully you will be able to find ways to reduce expenses so you can begin that process.

Are you already paying yourself first without knowing it

The first thing to understand is that you may already be paying yourself first whether you know it or not. And that is you may already have a 401(k) at work (or other pension plan) and may consider that as part of your budgeted accumulation for your future.

Although I have known 401(k) millionaires they are not that common. Those individuals were usually six figure earners who had most (if not all) of their investment in their company's own stock. Over the course of a thirty plus year career they accumulated several million dollars.

You may already have some cash value life insurance but not funding it beyond the minimum premium requirement; so it will never grow to a significant amount.

Thirty percent of U.S. households have no life insurance at all, and only 44 percent have individual life insurance. Fifty percent of U.S. households (58 million) say they need more life insurance. But the average amount of coverage for U.S. adults has fallen by thirty thousand dollars from a peak of $197,000 fifteen years ago.

And today four in ten households with children under 18 are headed by a single mother as the sole earner for her family. But women on average only have two-thirds the average coverage as men (life insurance as an investment will be addressed in Part 4).

You may already try and save some money for short-term goals. Remember the "vacation" and "new furniture" accounts?

Lastly, you may be saving money with the IRS! Yes, that annual tax refund is a deferred savings account without any earnings. I have known a number of households that deliberately withheld more in order to have a higher refund at tax time.

They do that because they understood themselves -- they know they would spend it if they had it all year in their paychecks. One of the reasons they would give me was that once it was withheld from their paycheck(s), they couldn't get it back until they filed their tax return. So they let the IRS become their annual savings account. Without having read this book they had implemented a form of paying themselves first.

These people were at least trying to control their spending during the year. Most did not put it into investments; rather, they accumulated the money in order to buy something special or go on a vacation.

Pretty good example of tough love.

Obstacles to Success

As I said in Chapter 2 being rich is a state of mind. But having true wealth requires more than a state of mind.

Right now you are reading this book because you have a desire to achieve a level of wealth to fund the personal financial goals you have for your life.

If you currently have a good income and are taking care of your daily needs for you and your family, drive a nice car, and live in a nice home, you may not be as concerned about the future.

You may think this is how it will always be. But...
...there will be many temptations for you and your spouse along the way to stop paying yourself first such as the following:

    1. Keeping up with the Jones's.

    2. I want it now!

    3. Expenses of having and raising children.

4. Taxes.

5. Changes in your income (downward).

I am sure there are more, but if you review these five you will find at least one or two that either already has or will impact your dedication to gaining wealth.

Numbers one and two are the worst of the list. Simply put, going without (or the perception of without) for the sake of having more way out in the future is a hard course to follow.

The principle of the first secret, Pay Yourself First, often requires you to find the money in your budget; or move it from one spending account to another.

But the most important thing it takes is YOU! It requires your commitment to a long term goal.

Looking in the Mirror Test

My last bit of advice is to simply look at yourself in the mirror, or together with your spouse, and ask this one question:

"Do I/we really want to attain wealth by the time I/we are sixty-five?"

If the answer is "Yes" then make a promise to yourself, or to your spouse, right in front of that mirror, to begin or increase the amount you are going to pay yourself first.

You will now have a covenant with yourself, or between you and your spouse, to do so.

Once you have done this, you are ready for the second and third secrets that follow.

Part 2
"The Second Secret"

It is reputed that the first person who said that compound interest was the Eighth Wonder of the World was Benjamin Franklin (late 1700's).

In the first edition of this book I gave that privilege to Baron Rothschild (mid-1800's).

But most people today prefer to say it was Albert Einstein (early 1900's) who said, "The most powerful force in the universe is compound interest."

There is really no proof that any of these statements were actually made by any of these people; but I am sure Einstein probably said it. He made many very observations on life, on love, and, of course, on how the universe works (his "General Theory of Relativity").

And it is also said that Einstein developed the "Rule of 72." That is an important financial predictor I will explain shortly.

By the end of Part 2 you will have a mathematical formula to accumulate great wealth. You will understand the second of three secrets, the most powerful of them all, but totally useless if you never use the first secret.

Are you going to use the first secret?

If so read on; if not you will simply let your lifetime of earnings slip through your fingers – just like sand.

"Nothing can be created from nothing."

- Titus Lucretius Carus (99-55 B.C.)

Chapter 4: Compound Interest

The second secret to accumulate wealth is compound interest. Many of you are already using it; but I doubt you can compute it or define it.

Let's examine three questions:

What is compound interest?

Why has it been called the "Eighth Wonder of the World?"

Why is it so important?

<u>Calculation of interest</u>

To begin let's understand simple interest.

Simple interest is simply a stated rate of return expressed as a percentage over the course of one year. It is the easiest to calculate.

For example, if you earn five percent (5%) interest on ten dollars of savings (say at a bank) left in your account for one year the interest amount earned on that ten dollars will be fifty cents.

Your account balance at the end of the year will be $10.50. You earned 5% simple interest for one year.

For retired people, who often live on the interest earned on their savings, simple interest is all they will get. Generally, they will withdraw the interest (fifty cents) and leave the initial principle amount (ten dollars) in the account to earn the going rate of simple interest for the next year of retirement.

In this example they are said to be "living on the interest" and are totally dependent on the simple interest rate for their retirement income. Should it inadequate they may need to withdraw some funds from the account causing them to earn less interest during the next year as they would have less money in the account.

The rate the bank pays is market based and may go up; or may go down. As we all know now in 2018, the simple interest rate at a bank is very, very low (and has been for the past ten years).

Now let's understand compound interest.

If you leave the $10.50 from the prior example in your account where you earned the fifty cents of interest for the first year and continue to earn 5% simple interest in the second year, you will now have earned fifty-two and one-half cents at the end of the second year. The account balance will be $11.025.

We don't really have "half pennies" but I think you get the idea. Leave it a third year and you would earn fifty-five and one-eighth cents. Your account balance would now be $11.57625 in exact mathematical terms.

Compound interest is the repeated annual simple interest earned in an account where the prior year's earnings are left in the account as part of the next year's balance. Thus it "compounds" over time.

If this is beginning to sound complicated, IT IS! And that's because there are many ways to calculate compound interest: daily, weekly, monthly, quarterly, semi-annually, and annually. To calculate any of these rates involves some serious math. Thank goodness for computers and business calculators available today to do it.

In addition, most banks that pay annual interest on accounts where you have the ability to take out the money at will, only pay on either the average balance, or worse, on the lowest balance during the agreed cycle. That is why monthly interest is much better than annual interest. CD's pay over the agreed period of time and if you take it early there is an interest forfeiture penalty.

Lastly, you have probably seen the term APR, which stands for Annual Percentage Rate, on a loan or mortgage account, or a savings account.

It is a government requirement (called The Truth in Lending Act of 1968) for all banks and lenders to distill their proposed interest rate and time period down to a single APR so that you may compare one offer to another in the same mathematical context.

Once you understand compound interest there are two other concepts you need to understand. These two concepts allow you to compare the yields of totally different types of investments. They are:

1. Time value of money; and

2. Present value / future value.

These are key mathematical calculations that directly impact how you will be selecting a saving/investment amount now and how valuable that amount will be at a future date.

In other words, what would you pay for a future dollar today? Let's get started.

Time value of money is the effect that inflation has on a dollar. We all know that a dollar today generally does not buy as much as a dollar did ten or twenty years ago. And try a hundred years ago!

Inflation erodes the value of your savings and physical assets. To offset inflation, the earnings on your investments must be equal to or greater than the inflation rate. Thus the time value of money is the earned interest rate minus the inflation rate for a net gain or loss in purchasing power.

Present value and future value is more complex than any other aspect of this chapter. Basically present value is the value in today's dollars of future dollars.

What?

Let's use an example. If I said I would give you ten dollars in ten years if you gave me five dollars today; or twenty dollars in twenty years for four dollars today, which one is the better deal for you? (I am assuming you can wait for the payoff.)

Hint: this is not a trick question. It can be solved quickly with the Rule of 72 (remember Albert Einstein created this rule).

The Rule of 72 says a dollar doubles to two dollars over the number of years equal to 72 divided by the earning/interest rate expressed as a percent.

The reverse of this statement is that if you divide the current earning/interest rate by 72 the result equals the number of years it takes to double the dollar.

The Rule of 72 is quite accurate for normal time intervals and nominal interest rates.

Okay, back to my proposition. Assuming you want the highest APR on your investment, which one would you choose?

In the first offer, the five dollars doubled in ten years. So 72 divided by 10 is 7.2% APR.

In the second offer, using an APR of 7.2% (the rate from the first offer) the four dollars would double to eight in ten years, and then double again to sixteen dollars by twenty years. But I offered you twenty dollars at twenty years. That is more than sixteen dollars so the second offer has to have a higher earnings/interest rate. Do you agree?

It actually takes a formula to solve the second offer correctly, but you can quickly see that second offer more than doubled so the rate had to be greater than 7.2%. The actual rate is 8.4%.

Therefore, the second offer was better (it has a higher APR). This simple example is actually a present value analysis to guide you to the best decision on two unequal investment choices.

Now let's understand present value comparisons.

Back to the proposition. If I did the math on the first offer for twenty years, the interval of the second offer, what amount did you get?

Twenty dollars, right. Five became ten in ten years, amd if you allow it to double again in ten years it becomes twenty dollars.

Since both offers amounted to twenty dollars in twenty years, the one for which you paid the least is better, right?

The payment to me of four dollars is better than five dollars to have the same amount at the same point in the future.

The only variable excluded in this proposition is risk. That is because the person (investment product) making the promise was the same (me); therefore, the risk of non-payment was equal in either choice. How to factor risk takes even greater mathematics.

For most of us, however, future value is what we need to understand the best. Future value is designed to help us evaluate a series of payments (annual savings) over an extended period of time at a planned interest rate (earnings).

In other words, what will four dollars invested each year at 8.4% become in twenty years? Our principle investment will be $4 x 20 years, or $80. The question to answer is what will the future value of that cash flow become?

To answer that question you need a computer, or a very good business calculator, or a lot of time to punch in the numbers over and over.

When I gained my economics degree in 1966 we used printed discount tables and would estimate a rate of return and then go over and under (called iteration) until we had the answer. That was tedious. I really like my computer now.

Using an Excel spreadsheet I get the answer. $4 per year for 20 years at 8.4% will be an account value of $191.

What would it become if I waited thirty years? Half again more?

No, it would now become $488, more than double. The last ten years allowed the first ten years to keep on earning compound interest on an already larger sum plus my added annual $4.

Back once more to my original offer. What was the original $4 worth at 20 years and again at 30 years? Let's see.

We already solved the first part, the original $4 payment become $20 in twenty years. But if allowed to continue to thirty years at that internal rate of 8.4% it would become $45. Whereas the $5 offer would became $40 in thirty years.

So what have we learned?

TIME is everything. The longer you wait to take the money in the future the greater the amount becomes relative to a prior equal interval of time. The impact is huge.

Let's go back to the last proposition. What if I wait ten years to begin saving $4 a year at 8.4% and thus have only twenty years before I need it? The answer was that I would have $191.

But if I started ten years earlier when I had the full thirty years to wait, I would have $488. More than double!

And what if after twenty years I stopped putting in the $4 a year but let the then balance ride for ten more years? I would have $429.

I bet you didn't expect that it would be so close to the amount you get ($488) by continuing to invest the $4 each year for the last ten years.

If you dig into the problem you will find that the last $4 a year over ten years ($40) only became $59!

There is an old saying that the first ten years of saving for your retirement will generally create an amount equal to what you will have for saving the same amount for the rest of your working years.

TIME is your friend when you have it; your enemy when you don't!

Impact of paying yourself first

Let's examine the impact of paying yourself first. The chart on the next two pages (viewed side by side) is based on the assumption that you have been earning the average starting salary for a college graduate for forty years.

On the left page is the sum of saving 10% each year for those 40 years (Note: or any number of years less by looking at the cumulative amount).

Now clearly, that is not going to be your annual income forever. You will receive raises over time from two sources; COLAs (cost of living adjustments); and promotions.

Many individuals will be promoted faster than others and potentially to even higher salaries. Some will strike out on their own and start a small business (with a high risk of failure); and some will succeed in sales (usually the highest paying of all).

When you look at a chart or table of averages it is just that -- the average outcome for a large group of people from the highest one to the lowest one. It will never be exactly you; you will be higher; or lower; or up and down over your lifetime.

But the principle is the same. Pay yourself first no matter what you earn; and over the years find a way to increase it to even more than ten present. You will be stunned at the outcome. I promise.

Remember my earlier disclaimer. I have reviewed dozens of sources, but the primary one is the DOL, Census Bureau, IRS, Congressional studies, and other open source data from the worldwide web.

Pay Yourself First -- 10% of the average 2015 starting salary of $45,478 for college graduates			Average annual raise over past 30 years 3%	
Time in Years	Annual Amount Saved	Cumulative Amount Saved	Annual Amount Saved	Cumulative Amount Saved
0				
1	$ 4,548	$ 4,548	$ 4,548	$ 4,548
2	$ 4,548	$ 9,096	$ 4,684	$ 9,232
3	$ 4,548	$ 13,644	$ 4,825	$ 14,057
4	$ 4,548	$ 18,192	$ 4,970	$ 19,027
5	$ 4,548	$ 22,740	$ 5,119	$ 24,146
6	$ 4,548	$ 27,288	$ 5,272	$ 29,418
7	$ 4,548	$ 31,836	$ 5,431	$ 34,849
8	$ 4,548	$ 36,384	$ 5,593	$ 40,442
9	$ 4,548	$ 40,932	$ 5,761	$ 46,204
10	$ 4,548	$ 45,480	$ 5,934	$ 52,138
11	$ 4,548	$ 50,028	$ 6,112	$ 58,250
12	$ 4,548	$ 54,576	$ 6,295	$ 64,545
13	$ 4,548	$ 59,124	$ 6,484	$ 71,030
14	$ 4,548	$ 63,672	$ 6,679	$ 77,709
15	$ 4,548	$ 68,220	$ 6,879	$ 84,588
16	$ 4,548	$ 72,768	$ 7,086	$ 91,673
17	$ 4,548	$ 77,316	$ 7,298	$ 98,972
18	$ 4,548	$ 81,864	$ 7,517	$ 106,489
19	$ 4,548	$ 86,412	$ 7,743	$ 114,232
20	$ 4,548	$ 90,960	$ 7,975	$ 122,206
21	$ 4,548	$ 95,508	$ 8,214	$ 130,421
22	$ 4,548	$ 100,056	$ 8,461	$ 138,881
23	$ 4,548	$ 104,604	$ 8,714	$ 147,596
24	$ 4,548	$ 109,152	$ 8,976	$ 156,572
25	$ 4,548	$ 113,700	$ 9,245	$ 165,817
26	$ 4,548	$ 118,248	$ 9,523	$ 175,339
27	$ 4,548	$ 122,796	$ 9,808	$ 185,147
28	$ 4,548	$ 127,344	$ 10,102	$ 195,250
29	$ 4,548	$ 131,892	$ 10,405	$ 205,655
30	$ 4,548	$ 136,440	$ 10,718	$ 216,373
31	$ 4,548	$ 140,988	$ 11,039	$ 227,412
32	$ 4,548	$ 145,536	$ 11,370	$ 238,783
33	$ 4,548	$ 150,084	$ 11,711	$ 250,494
34	$ 4,548	$ 154,632	$ 12,063	$ 262,557
35	$ 4,548	$ 159,180	$ 12,425	$ 274,982
36	$ 4,548	$ 163,728	$ 12,797	$ 287,779
37	$ 4,548	$ 168,276	$ 13,181	$ 300,960
38	$ 4,548	$ 172,824	$ 13,577	$ 314,537
39	$ 4,548	$ 177,372	$ 13,984	$ 328,521
40	$ 4,548	$ 181,920	$ 14,404	$ 342,925

	3%	5%		7%		9%	
Time in years	Annual Amount Invested	Annual Rate of Return	Account Balance (EOY)	Annual Rate of Return	Account Balance (EOY)	Annual Rate of Return	Account Balance (EOY)
0							
1	$ 4,548	$ -	$ 4,548	$ -	$ 4,548	$ -	$ 4,548
2	$ 4,684	$ 227	$ 9,460	$ 318	$ 9,551	$ 409	$ 9,642
3	$ 4,825	$ 473	$ 14,758	$ 669	$ 15,044	$ 868	$ 15,334
4	$ 4,970	$ 738	$ 20,465	$ 1,053	$ 21,067	$ 1,380	$ 21,684
5	$ 5,119	$ 1,023	$ 26,608	$ 1,475	$ 27,661	$ 1,952	$ 28,755
6	$ 5,272	$ 1,330	$ 33,210	$ 1,936	$ 34,869	$ 2,588	$ 36,615
7	$ 5,431	$ 1,661	$ 40,301	$ 2,441	$ 42,741	$ 3,295	$ 45,341
8	$ 5,593	$ 2,015	$ 47,910	$ 2,992	$ 51,326	$ 4,081	$ 55,015
9	$ 5,761	$ 2,395	$ 56,067	$ 3,593	$ 60,680	$ 4,951	$ 65,728
10	$ 5,934	$ 2,803	$ 64,804	$ 4,248	$ 70,862	$ 5,915	$ 77,577
11	$ 6,112	$ 3,240	$ 74,156	$ 4,960	$ 81,934	$ 6,982	$ 90,671
12	$ 6,295	$ 3,708	$ 84,160	$ 5,735	$ 93,965	$ 8,160	$ 105,127
13	$ 6,484	$ 4,208	$ 94,852	$ 6,578	$ 107,027	$ 9,461	$ 121,073
14	$ 6,679	$ 4,743	$ 106,274	$ 7,492	$ 121,198	$ 10,897	$ 138,649
15	$ 6,879	$ 5,314	$ 118,466	$ 8,484	$ 136,561	$ 12,478	$ 158,006
16	$ 7,086	$ 5,923	$ 131,475	$ 9,559	$ 153,206	$ 14,221	$ 179,312
17	$ 7,298	$ 6,574	$ 145,347	$ 10,724	$ 171,229	$ 16,138	$ 202,749
18	$ 7,517	$ 7,267	$ 160,132	$ 11,986	$ 190,732	$ 18,247	$ 228,513
19	$ 7,743	$ 8,007	$ 175,881	$ 13,351	$ 211,826	$ 20,566	$ 256,822
20	$ 7,975	$ 8,794	$ 192,650	$ 14,828	$ 234,628	$ 23,114	$ 287,911
21	$ 8,214	$ 9,633	$ 210,497	$ 16,424	$ 259,266	$ 25,912	$ 322,037
22	$ 8,461	$ 10,525	$ 229,482	$ 18,149	$ 285,876	$ 28,983	$ 359,481
23	$ 8,714	$ 11,474	$ 249,671	$ 20,011	$ 314,601	$ 32,353	$ 400,549
24	$ 8,976	$ 12,484	$ 271,130	$ 22,022	$ 345,599	$ 36,049	$ 445,574
25	$ 9,245	$ 13,557	$ 293,932	$ 24,192	$ 379,037	$ 40,102	$ 494,921
26	$ 9,523	$ 14,697	$ 318,151	$ 26,533	$ 415,092	$ 44,543	$ 548,987
27	$ 9,808	$ 15,908	$ 343,867	$ 29,056	$ 453,956	$ 49,409	$ 608,204
28	$ 10,102	$ 17,193	$ 371,163	$ 31,777	$ 495,836	$ 54,738	$ 673,044
29	$ 10,405	$ 18,558	$ 400,126	$ 34,708	$ 540,950	$ 60,574	$ 744,024
30	$ 10,718	$ 20,006	$ 430,850	$ 37,866	$ 589,534	$ 66,962	$ 821,704
31	$ 11,039	$ 21,543	$ 463,432	$ 41,267	$ 641,840	$ 73,953	$ 906,696
32	$ 11,370	$ 23,172	$ 497,974	$ 44,929	$ 698,139	$ 81,603	$ 999,669
33	$ 11,711	$ 24,899	$ 534,584	$ 48,870	$ 758,721	$ 89,970	$ 1,101,351
34	$ 12,063	$ 26,729	$ 573,376	$ 53,110	$ 823,894	$ 99,122	$ 1,212,535
35	$ 12,425	$ 28,669	$ 614,470	$ 57,673	$ 893,991	$ 109,128	$ 1,334,088
36	$ 12,797	$ 30,723	$ 657,990	$ 62,579	$ 969,368	$ 120,068	$ 1,466,953
37	$ 13,181	$ 32,900	$ 704,071	$ 67,856	$ 1,050,405	$ 132,026	$ 1,612,161
38	$ 13,577	$ 35,204	$ 752,852	$ 73,528	$ 1,137,510	$ 145,094	$ 1,770,832
39	$ 13,984	$ 37,643	$ 804,478	$ 79,626	$ 1,231,120	$ 159,375	$ 1,944,191
40	$ 14,404	$ 40,224	$ 859,106	$ 86,178	$ 1,331,702	$ 174,977	$ 2,133,572
	$ 342,925	$516,181		$988,777		$ 1,790,647	

51

Once again, the chart on the left prior page is the total value of paying yourself first. The left column is the pure amount of ten percent (10%) of your starting salary, and the right column is your starting salary with an average increase (raise) of three percent (3%) which has been the generally accepted average for the past thirty years.

The right page of this chart is investing ten percent of your future salary earnings with increases of three percent per year then earning three different rates of return: 5%; 7%; and 9%.

The primary purpose of the chart is to so show the power of compound interest over a range of rates that are historically capable of being achieved over the long haul (more in Part 5).

For now, it is useful to go through these charts and apply them to your own situation.

If you do not have forty years left, just go to the number of years you do have left and see what you would have.

If you earn more than the amount shown on the chart, just multiply what you currently earn by 10% and then divide that by the number at the beginning of the chart (4,548). Then multiply that factor times the total dollar result in the cumulative column for the number of years you have left (an example is shown at the end of the second chart.)

For example, in the first chart, if you are 45 years old and want to retire at 65 multiply your current annual income by 10% and then divide that by 4,548. Then take that factor and multiple the future account balance on the chart for year 20 and that should be the amount you have saved with normal raises.

You can do the same on the second chart for different investment rates too.

Conclusion

Compound interest is powerful. Albert Einstein was right about that.

And with enough time it can become a number beyond belief. That is why trust fund babies are so fortunate. They get a 21-year head start on the rest of us.

I waited until age 29; and, unfortunately, most of you will wait.

But if you are in your twenties right now and you are reading this book, please realize you hold the power to become very wealthy by age sixty or older if you really want it.

And if you are reading this book and are older and have children in or under their twenties, you hold that power for them by starting a small contribution for them today.

I will address this concept in the final chapter. But trust me, if you are a parent or grandparent and want to secure your progeny's future, put some money away where they can't get it (or even keep it a secret from them), and you will give them an asset one day of wealth beyond even their wildest dreams.

You can become a dream maker for them.

"Do you know what happens when you give a procrastinator a good idea? Nothing."

- Donald Gardner (no data)

"Do it now. Sometimes 'later' becomes 'never'."

- Unknown

Chapter 5: Delay -- the most costly thing you can do

At the end of Chapter 3 was a list of obstacles that may keep you from implementing the first secret.

The true cause of that list may simply be stated in one word -- procrastination. Webster's defines procrastination as:

: to be slow or late about doing something that should be done.

: to delay doing something until a later time because you do not want to do it.

: Synonyms: delay, retard, slow, slacken, detain.

<u>The price of delay</u>

I prefer to use the synonym "delay" for procrastination. I feel it most clearly embodies the impact of the lost time value of money by delaying the implementation of paying yourself first.

Secondarily, if you find yourself entering the middle to later years of your working life before you start, you will be well behind in the use of compound interest. This will either require a much larger contribution into your investment accounts; or you may be tempted to make high risk investments in the hope of catching up.

I will address this in Part 3, but for now, I simply want to mathematically show you the impact of delay on the time value of money.

The following chart (side by side on next two pages) allows you to enter it at any point and graphically see the impact of time on annual contributions. By starting late, paying yourself first 10% of your salary is better than not; however, you will be far behind compared to starting earlier.

Age in Years	Time in Years	Annual Amount Invested (1)	Annual Earnings (2)	End of Year Account Balance (3)	NOTES:
25	0				
26	1	$ 5,256	$ -	$ 5,256	(1) Annual
27	2	$ 5,414	$ 368	$ 11,038	Amount
28	3	$ 5,576	$ 773	$ 17,386	Invested
29	4	$ 5,743	$ 1,217	$ 24,347	is ten
30	5	$ 5,916	$ 1,704	$ 31,967	percent
31	6	$ 6,093	$ 2,238	$ 40,297	(10%) of
32	7	$ 6,276	$ 2,821	$ 49,394	average
33	8	$ 6,464	$ 3,458	$ 59,316	starting
34	9	$ 6,658	$ 4,152	$ 70,126	salary for
35	10	$ 6,858	$ 4,909	$ 81,893	a college
36	11	$ 7,064	$ 5,733	$ 94,689	graduate
37	12	$ 7,276	$ 6,628	$ 108,593	in 2017
38	13	$ 7,494	$ 7,602	$ 123,688	and
39	14	$ 7,719	$ 8,658	$ 140,065	grows at
40	15	$ 7,950	$ 9,805	$ 157,820	3% per
41	16	$ 8,189	$ 11,047	$ 177,056	year
42	17	$ 8,434	$ 12,394	$ 197,884	(average historical
43	18	$ 8,687	$ 13,852	$ 220,423	raise).
44	19	$ 8,948	$ 15,430	$ 244,801	(2)
45	20	$ 9,216	$ 17,136	$ 271,154	Annual
46	21	$ 9,493	$ 18,981	$ 299,627	Earnings
47	22	$ 9,778	$ 20,974	$ 330,379	forecast
48	23	$ 10,071	$ 23,127	$ 363,576	to be 7%
49	24	$ 10,373	$ 25,450	$ 399,400	(average historical
50	25	$ 10,684	$ 27,958	$ 438,042	rate of
51	26	$ 11,005	$ 30,663	$ 479,710	return of
52	27	$ 11,335	$ 33,580	$ 524,625	the stock
53	28	$ 11,675	$ 36,724	$ 573,024	market).
54	29	$ 12,025	$ 40,112	$ 625,161	(3) End of
55	30	$ 12,386	$ 43,761	$ 681,308	Year
56	31	$ 12,758	$ 47,692	$ 741,757	account balance
57	32	$ 13,140	$ 51,923	$ 806,821	assumes
58	33	$ 13,535	$ 56,477	$ 876,833	invest-
59	34	$ 13,941	$ 61,378	$ 952,152	ments
60	35	$ 14,359	$ 66,651	$ 1,033,161	made at
61	36	$ 14,790	$ 72,321	$ 1,120,272	the end
62	37	$ 15,233	$ 78,419	$ 1,213,925	of each year.
63	38	$ 15,690	$ 84,975	$ 1,314,590	
64	39	$ 16,161	$ 92,021	$ 1,422,772	
65	40	$ 16,646	$ 99,594	$ 1,539,012	
		$ 396,309	$ 1,142,703		

Time in Years	Annual Amount Invested (1)	Annual Earnings (2)	End of Year Account Balance (3)	Time in Years	Annual Amount Invested (1)	Annual Earnings (2)	End of Year Account Balance (3)
	Initial amount is based on salary after ten years of raises						
0	$ 6,858		$ 6,858				
1	$ 7,064	$ 480	$ 14,402		Initial amount is based on salary after twenty years of raises		
2	$ 7,276	$ 1,008	$ 22,686				
3	$ 7,494	$ 1,588	$ 31,767				
4	$ 7,719	$ 2,224	$ 41,710				
5	$ 7,950	$ 2,920	$ 52,580				
6	$ 8,189	$ 3,681	$ 64,449				
7	$ 8,434	$ 4,511	$ 77,395				
8	$ 8,688	$ 5,418	$ 91,500				
9	$ 8,948	$ 6,405	$ 106,854				
10	$ 9,217	$ 7,480	$ 123,550	0	$ 9,216		$ 9,216
11	$ 9,493	$ 8,648	$ 141,692	1	$ 9,492	$ 645	$ 19,354
12	$ 9,778	$ 9,918	$ 161,388	2	$ 9,777	$ 1,355	$ 30,486
13	$ 10,071	$ 11,297	$ 182,756	3	$ 10,071	$ 2,134	$ 42,690
14	$ 10,373	$ 12,793	$ 205,922	4	$ 10,373	$ 2,988	$ 56,051
15	$ 10,685	$ 14,415	$ 231,022	5	$ 10,684	$ 3,924	$ 70,659
16	$ 11,005	$ 16,172	$ 258,198	6	$ 11,004	$ 4,946	$ 86,609
17	$ 11,335	$ 18,074	$ 287,607	7	$ 11,335	$ 6,063	$ 104,006
18	$ 11,675	$ 20,133	$ 319,415	8	$ 11,675	$ 7,280	$ 122,961
19	$ 12,026	$ 22,359	$ 353,800	9	$ 12,025	$ 8,607	$ 143,593
20	$ 12,386	$ 24,766	$ 390,952	10	$ 12,386	$ 10,052	$ 166,030
21	$ 12,758	$ 27,367	$ 431,076	11	$ 12,757	$ 11,622	$ 190,410
22	$ 13,141	$ 30,175	$ 474,392	12	$ 13,140	$ 13,329	$ 216,878
23	$ 13,535	$ 33,207	$ 521,135	13	$ 13,534	$ 15,181	$ 245,594
24	$ 13,941	$ 36,479	$ 571,555	14	$ 13,940	$ 17,192	$ 276,725
25	$ 14,359	$ 40,009	$ 625,923	15	$ 14,358	$ 19,371	$ 310,454
26	$ 14,790	$ 43,815	$ 684,528	16	$ 14,789	$ 21,732	$ 346,975
27	$ 15,234	$ 47,917	$ 747,678	17	$ 15,233	$ 24,288	$ 386,496
28	$ 15,691	$ 52,337	$ 815,706	18	$ 15,690	$ 27,055	$ 429,240
29	$ 16,161	$ 57,099	$ 888,967	19	$ 16,160	$ 30,047	$ 475,447
30	$ 16,646	$ 62,228	$ 967,841	20	$ 16,645	$ 33,281	$ 525,374
	$ 342,918	$ 624,922			$ 264,282	$ 261,091	

How much does it take to catch up? The following chart shows how much of your future paycheck would be required to catch-up at age 35 and at 45 (to equal the future amount by starting at age 25).

Time in Years	Annual Amount Invested (1)	Annual Earnings (remains at 7%)	End of Year Account Balance	Time in Years	Annual Amount Invested (2)	Annual Earnings (remains at 7%)	End of Year Account Balance
0	$ 10,906		$				
1	$ 11,233	$ 763	$				
2	$ 11,570	$ 1,603	$				
3	$ 11,917	$ 2,525	$				
4	$ 12,275	$ 3,536	$				
5	$ 12,643	$ 4,643	$ 85,010				
6	$ 13,022	$ 5,853	$ 102,491				
7	$ 13,413	$ 7,174	$ 123,079				
8	$ 13,815	$ 8,616	$ 145,509				
9	$ 14,230	$ 10,186	$ 169,925				
10	$ 14,657	$ 11,895	$ 196,477	0	$ 26,998		$ 26,998
11	$ 15,096	$ 13,753	$ 225,326	1	$ 27,808	$ 1,890	$ 56,696
12	$ 15,549	$ 15,773	$ 256,649	2	$ 28,642	$ 3,969	$ 89,307
13	$ 16,016	$ 17,965	$ 290,630	3	$ 29,501	$ 6,251	$ 125,060
14	$ 16,496	$ 20,344	$ 327,470	4	$ 30,386	$ 8,754	$ 164,200
15	$ 16,991	$ 22,923	$ 367,384	5	$ 31,298	$ 11,494	$ 206,992
16	$ 17,501	$ 25,717	$ 410,602	6	$ 32,237	$ 14,489	$ 253,719
17	$ 18,026	$ 28,742	$ 457,370	7	$ 33,204	$ 17,760	$ 304,683
18	$ 18,567	$ 32,016	$ 507,953	8	$ 34,200	$ 21,328	$ 360,211
19	$ 19,124	$ 35,557	$ 562,633	9	$ 35,226	$ 25,215	$ 420,652
20	$ 19,697	$ 39,384	$ 621,715	10	$ 36,283	$ 29,446	$ 486,381
21	$ 20,288	$ 43,520	$ 685,523	11	$ 37,372	$ 34,047	$ 557,799
22	$ 20,897	$ 47,987	$ 754,407	12	$ 38,493	$ 39,046	$ 635,338
23	$ 21,524	$ 52,808	$ 828,740	13	$ 39,647	$ 44,474	$ 719,459
24	$ 22,170	$ 58,012	$ 908,921	14	$ 40,837	$ 50,362	$ 810,658
25	$ 22,835	$ 63,624	$ 995,380	15	$ 42,062	$ 56,746	$ 909,466
26	$ 23,520	$ 69,677	$ 1,088,577	16	$ 43,324	$ 63,663	$ 1,016,453
27	$ 24,225	$ 76,200	$ 1,189,002	17	$ 44,624	$ 71,152	$ 1,132,228
28	$ 24,952	$ 83,230	$ 1,297,185	18	$ 45,962	$ 79,256	$ 1,257,446
29	$ 25,701	$ 90,803	$ 1,413,688	19	$ 47,341	$ 88,021	$ 1,392,809
30	$ 26,472	$ 98,958	$ 1,539,118	20	$ 48,761	$ 97,497	$ 1,539,067
	$ 545,329	$ 993,789			$ 774,208	$ 764,859	

(1) Initial amount is 15.9% of salary

(2) Initial amount is 29.3% of salary

The percentage of your income needed at age 35 (using the future income forecast at that age of $59,340 is 15.9% (9436/59340).

The percentage of your income needed at age 45 (using the future income forecast at that age of $79,750 is 35.6% (28360/79750).

I doubt that the average person can suddenly begin saving that amount of each paycheck at that age. So, once again, it's simple; if you just don't get around to it you may never be able to catch up.

Why people delay

Your enemy is *your ability* to live on your actual income, whatever that may be, and not get "around to it."

If you simply "bite the bullet" as they say in old Western movies before the pain starts, and begin with some amount of contribution from your paycheck, I promise you will figure out how to live on the remainder.

And then, as you accommodate that investment amount, and get a raise, I suggest that you always divide that raise into three parts:

1. One-third for taxes;

2. One-third for you and your family; and

3. One-third to an increase in what you pay yourself first.

Lastly, I have previously mentioned that if you do a budget analysis you will probably find areas that you can reduce. One of the most common is "eating out."

Yes, it is nice to have dinner out with your spouse; or your family. But consider two things.

First, how often do you do it? If often, and in lieu of cooking at home at the end of a busy day, can you reduce that?

Second, do you order alcoholic drinks? I have no issue with drinking alcohol, but what you pay for alcoholic drinks when you dine out is usually way more than the value you receive.

There is an old saying that goes, "I have champagne taste on a beer budget."

There is nothing to be ashamed about for trimming your lifestyle. Paying yourself first will secure your ability to reach retirement and then you can afford not only champagne, but a wonderful retirement home in which to store the bottles.

Part 3
"The Third Secret"

What if you could invest in a venture and have a partner who would assist you? A partner who would either share some of the risk; or enhance your gains; or even do both.

The third secret is that such a partner does exists. That partner is called "Uncle Sam."

Now you may not like it that you have Uncle Sam as your partner as many people dislike the IRS and the U.S. tax code. But the simply reality is that you cannot avoid having Uncle Sam in your life if you are an American citizen or resident alien.

As Benjamin Franklin so aptly stated: "There are only two certainties in life -- death and taxes."

So why fight the system? The third secret is about how to reduce, avoid, or delay federal income taxes to your advantage.

The U.S. tax code is riddled with loopholes for the wealthy and corporations, but it also has a good number of opportunities for the "little guy." (Note: that's you and me.)

What is the U.S. Income Tax Code?

The first income tax was passed in 1862 under President Abraham Lincoln to support the cost of the Civil War. It was 3% on income between $600 and $10,000; and a higher rate of 5% on incomes over $10,000. It was terminated in 1872.

Later, this same tax was imposed in 1894 but in 1895 the Supreme Court ruled that it was unconstitutional.

In 1913 the income tax became permanent when congress and the states ratified the 16th Amendment to the Constitution. This amendment gave congress the power to set tax rates and pass laws to compute what you owe; and we have had an income tax ever since.

The current income tax is based on a totally revised set of laws passed by congress known as The Internal Revenue Code of 1954. That is the "chassis" upon which all changes have been made to date.

This chassis is still there even after the new tax reform law passed in 2017 known as the Tax Cuts and Jobs Act effective on January 1, 2018. Politicians always tie tax bills to jobs since 1981.

In 1981 President Reagan pressed congress to pass the largest tax cuts in the history of the income tax. This bill was The Economic Recovery Tax Act of 1981 (ERTA).

The most important aspect of this bill was the lowering of the maximum tax rate to 50% (from 70%) and reducing the number of brackets from 25 to 14.

When I began my investing career in 1973 there were 25 brackets ranging from 14% to 70% (I was in the 42% bracket).

The most important thing that occurred in 1981 was the ability to write off investment expenses and all personal interest you paid from your other income (salaries, dividends, etc.).

Further, if an asset was sold after owning it one year, the entire gain was long-term capital gain of which 60% of the gain was excluded from taxation. The 40% left was treated as ordinary income.

The 1981 tax code created an immense opportunity in investment real estate. You could write off all of the expenses (including depreciation) against your regular income; and when you sold that asset the profit came back as long term capital gain (with only 40% of that gain taxed at your tax bracket).

The 1981 tax code made rental income real estate a pure tax avoidance generating money machine.

But then President Reagan changed his mind in 1986 and asked congress to amend the tax code with The Tax Reform Act of 1986 (TRA). That reform created the format for the Internal Revenue Code (IRC) as it stands today.

The most important thing this revision did was lower the top tax bracket from 50% to 38.5% with only 5 brackets. But, and there is always a "but," it radically changed what you could deduct.

First, the deduction for personal interest was eliminated (had a short phase out period) and the capital gains tax exclusion was eliminated. Instead, the long term capital gains maximum rate was set at 28%.

Second, on rental real estate you could no longer deduct the tax loss write-off (if any) if your income exceeded $150,000 (began to phase out at $100,000). And if you could deduct a loss it was capped at $25,000. This is still the way it is treated today.

As a result the rental real estate money machine was gone and this 1986 tax change caused a major depression in rental real estate values as the money from investors virtually dried up and many had to sell their properties to cover being upside down on cash flow.

After 1986 there have been five additional amendments to the TRA which has been now been amended again for tax year 2018 with the Tax Cut and Jobs Act of 2017.

Beginning in 2018 there are still seven tax brackets from 10% to a top of 37%. All sic brackets above 10% have been lowered either 2% or 3% each (see charts with explanations as you continue to read this section).

There are other important changes too, but for now you have the U.S. tax code (IRC) in a nutshell.

Even though politicians say each time there is a new tax law it makes it simpler, the implementation remains a mess.

As the great Greek philosopher Heraclitus (535-475 BC) said, "The only thing that is constant is change."

And Heraclitus lived in a far simpler time compared to what you and I have experienced since 1954's income tax.

What can come next?

What are the changes in the new 2018 tax law

Have you ever heard these two expressions: "Those who do not remember the past are doomed to repeat it;" and "It seems like déjà vu all over again?"

The last is from the humorous sayings of Yogi Berra; the first was said by George Santayana (1863-1952), a Spanish philosopher.

Before you can fully understand how to use the tax laws to help you, you must first understand the income tax system.

Other than raising revenue to fund the government, congress (and many state legislatures) uses the tax code to induce individuals and corporations to do things that you or they might not ordinarily do. It offers many forks in the road; which one will you take?

The government does this by putting incentives to reduce or offset what is owed as income tax into the tax code. By these incentives, you and I, or a corporation, may be willing to invest in one asset versus another asset.

NOTE: throughout this book the term asset means any one of the array of investments available to you. In the final assessment what you want is cash flow from your assets for reinvestment during your accumulation years; and income from your assets during your retirement years.

Cash flow only comes from two things: 1) your working income; or 2) the income generated from an asset you own (or upon its sale).

It is the cash flow from your assets that you will need to have in order to retire. And how much you have or don't have will depend on how you used the tax advantages available to you. The next chapter will address tax advantages in detail; but before we go there, you need to understand tax brackets.

What are tax brackets?

Tax Brackets in effect for 2017 are listed in this limited chart:

Tax Bracket	Taxable Income (Single)	Taxable Income (Married)
10%	$0 to $9,325	$0 to $18,650
15%	$9,326 to $37,950	$18,651 to $75,900
25%	$37,951 to $91,900	$75,901 to $153,100
28%	$91,901 to $191,650	$153,101 to $233,350
33%	$191,651 to $416,700	$233,351 to $416,700
35%	$416,700 to $418,400	$416,701 to $470,700
39.6%	$418,401 and over	$470,701 and over

Many people find tax brackets to be a very confusing topic. Before you can use them you must compute your taxable income. For example, a single person with a W-2 for $25,000 for the entire tax year with no extra deductions or investment income.

For the last fifty years, each taxpayer had a standard deduction and an exemption. In 2017 (the last year this applies) a single person had a standard deduction of $6,350 (every taxpayer is allowed this) to arrive at $18,650 of income ($25,000 minus $6,350) followed by a personal exemption deduction of $4,050 to arrive at $14,600 ($18,650 minus $4,050).

For married taxpayers filing together they would each have these same deductions. Assuming they both worked and made $50,000 ($25,000 each) they would have $12,700 as their combined standard deduction plus $8,100 for two exemptions resulting in a taxable income of $29,200 (double the single person). This is simple math.

One last example would be suppose that the above married couple had two children. They would also receive a personal exemption for each child of $4,050 for an addition deduction of $8,100 to arrive at a final taxable income of $21,100. This is how the tax system computed taxable income in 2017 and for over fifty years before that.

<u>Big changes for 2018</u>

But the new tax law changes this in a rather dramatic way. It has eliminated all personal exemptions.

In its place each taxpayer now has a standard deduction of $12,000. This is $1,600 more than the prior combined standard deduction of $6,350 plus the exemption of $4,050 of $12,400.

This is the first stage of providing all taxpayers a lower tax bill.

The next part of the 2018 tax law is lowering of the tax brackets. Compare this chart with the one for 2017.

Next, the brackets are expanded so that the same income in 2017 allocates a larger share of it into the lower brackets.

The net effect is an overall lowering of total taxes for *every* taxpayer at *every* level of income.

Tax Bracket	Taxable Income (Single)	Taxable Income (Married)
10%	$0 to $9,525	$0 to $19,050
12%	$9,526 to $38,700	$19,051 to $77,400
22%	$38,701 to $82,500	$77,401 to $165,000
24%	$82,501 to $157,500	$165,001 to $315,000
32%	$157,501 to $200,000	$315,001 to $400,000
35%	$200,001 to $500,000	$400,001 to $600,000
37%	$500,001 and over	$600,001 and over

BUT, here is another major change. What happened to the exemption for children? Or for a parent you support?

To offset the loss of that deduction from income the taxpayer(s) will now receive a tax credit of $2,000 for each eligible child (must live with you and be under age 17 during the tax year). The prior tax credit for eligible children was $1,000.

For a child who continues on to college the taxpayer(s) will receive a tax credit of $500 until that child reaches age 24 during the tax year (so long as they are still in college).

This same $500 tax credit is also granted for your parent(s) if you support them and there are other individuals who may qualify for this same credit when in the past they qualified as an exemption (but I am not addressing that here).

So can you say you are getting a tax reduction in 2018 compared to 2017.?

Yes, BUT…

…and there is always a "But."

Because of the larger standard deduction taxpayer(s) who itemize still have to exceed the standard deduction and since that nearly doubled from 2017 to 2018 and after many who did itemize will no longer do so. If your mortgage interest is low or the size of your mortgage is low you may have only been exceeding the past standard deduction by several thousand dollars. Now you will not itemize as the much higher standard deduction will exceed your itemized total.

Further, the combined deduction of property taxes on your residence plus either sales tax paid or state income taxes paid is now capped at $10,000. Many higher income taxpayers living in high income tax states will clearly be impacted.

People often talk about how much income tax they pay and confuse their tax bracket with what is actually paid. What is actually paid is called the effective tax rate on their total income.

For the single person identified earlier on page 66 with a taxable income of $14,600, he or she was in the 15% tax bracket, but the effective tax rate was 6.93%.

The effective rate is computed by dividing the total income tax paid, $1,733, by the total W-2 income, $25,000 (1733/25000).

One more example, if this single person were to earn $1,000 more during the tax year, how much more tax would he or she pay?

Each of the last dollars earned are now in the 15% tax bracket. So the answer is $150. He or she remains in the 15% tax bracket; however, his or her effective tax rate increased to 7.53% (1883/26000).

When you are evaluating using tax advantages as a means to reduce taxes on investments, it is very important to understand that your tax bracket is a key number, especially as you may drop into a lower bracket using tax deductions or a higher bracket if they have extra earnings or gains.

It is also useful to understand your effective tax rate too. It is the true benchmark of your total tax burden on all of your income. Recall the chart shown earlier of the overall federal tax burden as a percentage of income.

With this understanding of tax brackets and tax rates let's begin our journey through the IRC's myriad of tax advantages in the next chapter.

"The art of taxation consists in so plucking the goose to obtain the largest amount of feathers with the least possible amount of hissing."

- Jean-Baptiste Colbert (1619 – 1683)

"Taxes are what we pay for civilized society."
- Justice Oliver Wendell Holmes, Jr. (1841- 1935)

Chapter 6: How the tax code helps you grow wealth

The U.S. Income Tax Code (IRC) as it applies to individuals is pretty straight forward. It basically contains two sets of opportunities for individuals to avoid or defer income taxes on their savings and investments to their advantage.

In the interest of simplicity (this is not a text book) I am dividing the major ways for an individual to accomplish this into two distinct groups: (1) tax advantages; and (2) tax preferences. After you study these two groups the distinction will become clear.

Tax Advantages

There are three fundamental tax advantages in the 1954 IRC that have remained essentially unchanged over all of the revisions and modifications that were outlined in the initial discussion at the beginning of Part 3. They are:

1. Deduction of the invested dollars.

2. Deferral on the gain (appreciation) of the invested dollars.

3. Tax-free withdrawal of the deferred gains (appreciation).

Generally, you are allowed only two of these three in concert. As such a host of different investment structures have emerged to access these advantages providing different value to different individuals.

I will share more on this topic after a brief outline of tax preferences.

Tax Preferences

There are three tax preferences in the 1954 IRC that many duals use once they have acquired wealth.

They have not been changed in principle over time whenever congress revises the IRC; only on rates or specific assets affected.

These three tax preferences are:

1. Tax free earnings on state and local government issued bonds (aka Muni's).
2. Maximum tax rate on long-term capital gains.
3. Specific assets subject to capital gains treatment versus ordinary income treatment.

Generally, tax preferences reduce or avoid current tax. There is no limit on their use and they provide different value to different individuals based on an individual's tax bracket.

Briefly, a Muni-bond is exempt from federal income tax, but not state income tax, unless you live in the state of issue. To be of value Muni-bond holders should be in a high tax bracket; they are of little use to someone in a low tax bracket as they tend to pay a lower interest rate than corporate bonds that are taxable.

The maximum rate on capital gains has been all over the board over the past forty years. It was 20% in 2016-17, and 15% just a few years ago for nearly 14 years (and zero for low income taxpayers). It was 28% before that; and way back it was one-half of the individual's tax rate (computed by taxing only 50% of the gain), and for a brief period it taxed only 40% of the gain.

The 2018 Tax Cuts and Jobs Act established a new process for taxing long term capital gains based on taxable income. It can be a bit confusing but the chart looks like this:

Long-Term Capital Gains Rate	Single Taxpayers	Married Filing Jointly	Head of Household	Married Filing Separately
0%	Up to $38,600	Up to $77,200	Up to $51,700	Up to $38,600
15%	$38,600-$425,800	$77,200-$479,000	$51,700-$452,400	$38,600-$239,500
20%	Over $425,800	Over $479,000	Over $452,400	Over $239,500

Assets subject to capital gains tax include anything that has increased in value from the time of acquisition to the time of sale.

For example, if you buy a share of stock for $5 and hold it 150 days and then sell it for $10 you have made a gain of $5. Since it was not held for a year and a day (366 days) it is considered to be a short-term capital gain and is taxed as ordinary income; in other words at the tax bracket rate your income has reached.

If that same share had been held for 366 days or more and then sold it would be long-term capital gain and subject to taxation as shown in the table above.

Additionally, qualified dividends on stock of U.S. companies are taxed at the long-term capital gains rate. This is a great tax preference for wealthy individuals who have lots of income and lots of dividends.

If you own a home and sell it at a gain you have a capital gain. Based on how long you owned it, and if it was your principal residence, you have an exclusion of $250,000 if single and $500,000 if married. If the gain is more than that you would pay tax at the rate shown in the chart.

One other tax preference for only the *uber* wealthy is the carried interest for hedge fund managers. That income is only taxed as capital gains -- not as earned ordinary income.

This has been a brief discussion of some tax preferences; now let's return to tax advantages.

Tax Advantages (continued)

Let's now return the three fundamental tax advantages contained in the IRC.

Deduction of invested dollars.

The easiest way to understand this is either a 401(k) pension plan (and all of its relatives like a 403(b), etc.), or a Traditional IRA.

All of these retirement assets allow you to deduct the contribution you make during the tax year (subject to limits based on your income) so that you do not pay income tax on that money.

If you contribute $1,000 to a Traditional IRA, you deduct that from your other income on your tax return. If you are in the 12% tax bracket you save paying $120 in taxes for that year.

If you contribute to a 401(k) at work that contribution is excluded from your taxable income on your W-2. Your employer pays that amount directly to the trustee of the plan.

In both instances, however, you still pay Social Security taxes before the deduction for income tax is applied.

<u>Deferral on the gain (appreciation) of an asset.</u>

To continue with the Traditional IRA or your 401(k) at work, the money you contribute is then invested in various assets like stocks and bonds, or even gold or real estate.

If there are any earnings such as dividends from stock, interest from bonds, or capital gains whenever the plan manager sells stocks or bonds at a higher value than paid, all of these normally taxable events are deferred within the plan.

As an example, if you buy a stock directly in your personal stock account with a broker, and it pays a dividend, you then declare that dividend income on your tax return.

If the dividend income were "qualified" it would have a tax preference of not paying more than the long-term capital gains rate (again as shown in the previous chart).

As stock grows in value and you do not sell it, you have a deferred gain. You do not pay tax until you actually sell it.

Deferral is an intermediate benefit allowing you to hold assets over time and not pay tax on their increased value until you sell them.

Once you sell a capital asset, if you held it the required time to qualify as a long-term capital asset, you have a tax preference of paying long-term capital gains tax versus ordinary income tax on that gain. For higher income taxpayers this is a great advantage.

<u>Tax-free withdrawal of deferred gain.</u>

This tax advantage is the holy grail of all tax advantages and is currently available in only three ways.

First, it is allowed on the earnings and gains within a Roth IRA or Roth 401(k).

Second, you may withdraw gains in the cash value inside a life insurance policy when taken as a loan.

Third, and very technical, you may rollover tax deferred money from a traditional IRA or 401(k) into a tax-qualified annuity and use those funds to directly pay for long-term nursing home care and not pay income tax on those payments.

This is a recent development in the past fifteen years and is an incredible gift form Uncle Sam. It is the only way you can actually obtain all three of the current tax advantages on any tax deductible and tax deferred asset.

Of course, you need to be "old" and "unable" to provide complete care for yourself. But for you youngsters reading this book it will happen to one half of your someday. So be prepared.

How tax advantages are combined

I stated earlier that you are allowed to use no more than two of the three fundamental tax advantages in concert (except for the third example in the previous paragraph). Allow me to elaborate.

In a Traditional IRA your contribution is tax deductible and all earnings and capital gains are deferred until you withdraw funds from the plan after retirement (age 59 ½). Then, the money withdrawn becomes taxable to you in the year of the distribution.

You have now used the first and second of the three fundamental tax advantages.

Conversely, if you made that same contribution into a Roth IRA or Roth 401(k), the contribution would NOT have been deductible; however, all of the earnings and capital gains would be deferred and when you withdraw money after retirement (age 59 ½) the distributions are tax free. You do not pay income tax at all.

You have used the second and third of the three fundamental tax advantages.

Traditional versus Roth IRAs

Which one is best? This is a big decision and there are two philosophies that apply.

First, will you retire and be in a lower tax bracket? If so, then the Traditional IRA may be better. But remember, retiring into a lower tax bracket simply means that you have less income than when you worked.

Second, in the Traditional IRA and 401(k) you must begin to take distributions when you are 70 ½. That is not true for a Roth. You never have to take any money out of a Roth. You can leave it as an income tax free estate asset to your heirs should you choose.

Further, you can take out your basis from a Roth IRA tax free prior to age 59 ½ (subject to the plan being at least five years old) and use that money any time if needed during your working years; for example, as a down payment on a house, for college expenses or for unexpected medical costs (or any other financial need).

You cannot do that with a 401(k) or Traditional IRA. Any distribution is taxable.

Upon analysis, I clearly recommend that you only use a Roth IRA (an exception for your 401(k) will be noted in Chapter 7). I base this on the chart on the next page as my proof.

The chart assumes a $1,000 annual contribution earning 7%.

The account balance is the same at the end for both the Roth and the Traditional IRA.

Then, for the Traditional IRA, I assume you will take the tax savings due to the deduction (at 22%) and invest them in a stock fund that also earns 7% but is taxable as you earn it over time.

Time in Years	End of Year IRA Account Balance	Tax Savings reinvested in Side Fund (22%)	Annual Earnings (7%)	Less Income Tax due on Earnings	End of Year Account Balance	Tax on Total Distribution of IRA (22%)	Gain in Roth over Traditional IRA
0							
1	$ 1,000	$ 220			$ 220	$ (220)	$ -
2	$ 2,070	$ 220	$ 15	$ (3)	$ 452	$ (455)	$ 4
3	$ 3,215	$ 220	$ 30	$ (7)	$ 695	$ (707)	$ 12
4	$ 4,440	$ 220	$ 45	$ (10)	$ 950	$ (977)	$ 27
5	$ 5,751	$ 220	$ 60	$ (13)	$ 1,217	$ (1,265)	$ 48
6	$ 7,153	$ 220	$ 75	$ (17)	$ 1,496	$ (1,574)	$ 78
7	$ 8,654	$ 220	$ 90	$ (20)	$ 1,786	$ (1,904)	$ 118
8	$ 10,260	$ 220	$ 105	$ (23)	$ 2,088	$ (2,257)	$ 170
9	$ 11,978	$ 220	$ 120	$ (26)	$ 2,401	$ (2,635)	$ 234
10	$ 13,816	$ 220	$ 135	$ (30)	$ 2,727	$ (3,040)	$ 313
11	$ 15,784	$ 220	$ 150	$ (33)	$ 3,064	$ (3,472)	$ 409
12	$ 17,888	$ 220	$ 165	$ (36)	$ 3,412	$ (3,935)	$ 523
13	$ 20,141	$ 220	$ 180	$ (40)	$ 3,773	$ (4,431)	$ 658
14	$ 22,550	$ 220	$ 195	$ (43)	$ 4,145	$ (4,961)	$ 816
15	$ 25,129	$ 220	$ 210	$ (46)	$ 4,529	$ (5,528)	$ 1,000
16	$ 27,888	$ 220	$ 225	$ (50)	$ 4,924	$ (6,135)	$ 1,211
17	$ 30,840	$ 220	$ 240	$ (53)	$ 5,331	$ (6,785)	$ 1,454
18	$ 33,999	$ 220	$ 255	$ (56)	$ 5,750	$ (7,480)	$ 1,730
19	$ 37,379	$ 220	$ 270	$ (59)	$ 6,181	$ (8,223)	$ 2,043
20	$ 40,995	$ 220	$ 285	$ (63)	$ 6,623	$ (9,019)	$ 2,396
21	$ 44,865	$ 220	$ 300	$ (66)	$ 7,077	$ (9,870)	$ 2,793
22	$ 49,006	$ 220	$ 315	$ (69)	$ 7,543	$ (10,781)	$ 3,239
23	$ 53,436	$ 220	$ 330	$ (73)	$ 8,020	$ (11,756)	$ 3,736
24	$ 58,177	$ 220	$ 345	$ (76)	$ 8,509	$ (12,799)	$ 4,290
25	$ 63,249	$ 220	$ 360	$ (79)	$ 9,010	$ (13,915)	$ 4,905
26	$ 68,676	$ 220	$ 375	$ (83)	$ 9,523	$ (15,109)	$ 5,586
27	$ 74,484	$ 220	$ 390	$ (86)	$ 10,047	$ (16,386)	$ 6,340
28	$ 80,698	$ 220	$ 405	$ (89)	$ 10,583	$ (17,753)	$ 7,171
29	$ 87,347	$ 220	$ 420	$ (92)	$ 11,130	$ (19,216)	$ 8,086
30	$ 94,461	$ 220	$ 435	$ (96)	$ 11,690	$ (20,781)	$ 9,092
31	$ 102,073	$ 220	$ 450	$ (99)	$ 12,261	$ (22,456)	$ 10,196
32	$ 110,218	$ 220	$ 465	$ (102)	$ 12,843	$ (24,248)	$ 11,405
33	$ 118,933	$ 220	$ 480	$ (106)	$ 13,438	$ (26,165)	$ 12,728
34	$ 128,259	$ 220	$ 495	$ (109)	$ 14,044	$ (28,217)	$ 14,173
35	$ 138,237	$ 220	$ 510	$ (112)	$ 14,662	$ (30,412)	$ 15,751
36	$ 148,913	$ 220	$ 525	$ (116)	$ 15,291	$ (32,761)	$ 17,470
37	$ 160,337	$ 220	$ 540	$ (119)	$ 15,932	$ (35,274)	$ 19,342
38	$ 172,561	$ 220	$ 555	$ (122)	$ 16,585	$ (37,963)	$ 21,378
39	$ 185,640	$ 220	$ 570	$ (125)	$ 17,250	$ (40,841)	$ 23,591
40	$ 199,635	$ 220	$ 585	$ (129)	$ 17,926	$ (43,920)	$ 25,994
		$ 8,800	$ 11,700	$ (2,574)	$ 17,926		
		A	+B	+C	=D		
IRA/ROTH Balance					+IRA side fund	-IRA tax	=ROTH gain

I assume you take a total withdrawal of the IRA account at age 65 and pay tax at 22% on the Traditional IRA but not on the Roth of course. (Note: that tax rate is actually low as that sum would most likely put you in an even higher tax bracket.)

Either way my point is made that the Roth IRA outperforms the Traditional IRA after tax, and you have the other management advantages of the Roth IRA that are not as generous or easy to do with a Traditional IRA.

In my opinion the only time a Traditional IRA is better than a Roth is when your working years are at a tax rate of 32% or higher and your retirement years are at a rate of 22% or below.

How are tax advantages *and* preferences combined?

I previously stated that you are allowed to use no more than two of the three fundamental tax advantages in concert (except for the nursing home annuity example in a previous paragraph).

But there are two other ways that you can combine one/two tax advantages with an additional tax preference for a potentially favorable outcome. Again allow me to elaborate.

Stocks and mutual funds.

When you directly own stocks or a mutual fund (either in a brokerage account or directly), you are able to use one of the fundamental tax advantages (tax deferral on unrealized gains).

NOTE: realized gains or losses occur when you sell a capital asset; unrealized gains or losses are your current positions in a capital asset vis-a-vis the current fair market value.

Then, if you hold the asset at least one year and a day before you sell it (current tax law), it becomes a long term capital gain subject to the current maximum capital gains tax rate. This tax rate was the second of three tax preferences I previously discussed.

To be clear, if you buy a stock and it goes up and you sell it in six months, your capital gain is considered ordinary income. It is simply added to your other income and taxed at your highest tax bracket for your total income in that year.

One other consideration is when you directly hold stock or a mutual fund and they pay dividends. That income would be reported on your tax return even if it remains in your account or buys additional shares.

If the source of the dividend is a U.S. based company it is called a "qualified" dividend and would be subject to being taxed at no higher a rate than the long-term capital gains rate. Any dividend that is not qualified is taxed as ordinary income.

The mutual fund will report those amounts as will a brokerage account. If you own the stock directly (you clip coupons) you can determine that from a list of domestic companies.

As you can see direct ownership of stocks and mutual funds afford you the ability to use both tax advantages and preferences to a major advantage based on the amount of your other income and your final taxable income (review the prior chart on page 73).

Rental Real Estate.

When you own a single-family house, or a duplex, or even a multiple unit apartment property, you are able to combine two tax advantages and one tax preference into that investment.

Just for discussion, assume you bought your first home in an average neighborhood and lived in it for several years. Then you were transferred.

You may be tempted to sell the house, especially if it has gone up in value, but you are aware that your type of house in your neighborhood has good long term appreciation potential and you know that it can be readily rented for an amount that you know would cover the mortgage, taxes and insurance.

This may be a tough decision. Who would look after the property? Do you and your wife need the proceeds as a down payment on the next house you buy? Etc.

But then you realize that you have also been paying yourself first in your 401(k) and a Roth IRA so you ask yourself: "Why don't we keep it and let it become a rental property? Be part of our investment portfolio."

How would that work?

First, let's be clear. Finding a reputable qualified property manager is easy and solves the problem of being a landlord. When I bought my first rental over thirty-five years ago I managed it. I became a landlord with all of the headaches.

Then I was transferred it was simple. Hire out that problem -- which I did. Allow me to safely say you do not want to be a landlord and the problem is easily solved with professional management.

Second, what are the tax advantages of rental real estate? There are three as follows:

1. You may be able to deduct up to $25,000 of operational losses from your income.

NOTE: recall I previously mentioned that if you earn over $100,000, by $150,000 your deduction will be phased out. BUT it is carried forward to the year that

82

you sell the property and deducted then no matter what your income. You get that deduction value, just later.

2. As the property appreciates over time that gain is deferred.

3. When the property is sold, any gain over your original cost basis is long-term capital gain.

Once your property is labeled an investment property versus personal property, unlike when you lived in the house, all repairs, maintenance, manager fees, property taxes, mortgage interest, fire insurance, etc. are deducted from the rental income and the net amount is either income or loss. You can even deduct homeowner's dues if you have them.

Next, you get a new tax break called depreciation. That is an imaginary allowance equal to essentially 3.64% of what you paid for the house (not the land) as an annual deduction against the rent. For the average situation, because of depreciation, you will most likely show a net tax loss that will save you taxes.

And all the time someone else is helping you pay your mortgage down while the property is slowing appreciating in value. That is a win-win.

Rental real estate has been called the "trifecta" of investments. You write off losses, defer gains, and then pay the capital gains tax when you sell.

But let me warn you. You will be tempted to sell out. Especially if you have a nice profit and want to spend it on some other adventure. I have seen this too many times.

But if you keep it long term (I held some of my houses for over twenty years) rental real estate can be one of the most profitable assets in your portfolio.

"I may be wrong in regard to any or all of them; but holding it a sound maxim, that it is better to be only sometimes right, than at all times wrong, so soon as I discover my opinions to be erroneous, I shall be ready to renounce them."

- Abraham Lincoln (1809 – 1865)

Whenever you find yourself on the side of the majority, it is time to pause and reflect.

- Mark Twain (1835 – 1910)

We all have big changes in our lives that are more or less a second chance.

- Harrison Ford (1942 -)

Part 4
A change of mind

I have a confession to make. I have made many mistakes over the past forty-five years.

Paying myself first was not one of them, I faithfully did that; rather, trying to get rich quick was often my mistake.

I have been to just about every type of investment seminar there has ever been in the past.

I have read dozens upon dozens of books on investments.

And I have chased tax advantages for the sake of the tax benefit.

From it all I have learned this one thing:

NOTHING WORKS BUT PAYING YOURSELF FIRST

Getting Rich Quick

I am sure you have heard radio ads or TV commercials about the guy or gal who couldn't pay the electric bill and then he or she discovered how to flip houses and is now fabulously wealthy.

Or someone who developed a proprietary software system that only picks stocks that go up.

Or the guy who blah, blah, blah.

Before you go to any of these people's seminars or websites and buy their software or subscribe to their proprietary system or newsletters, ask yourself this one very important question:

"If I had a secret/special system that made me a multi-millionaire in the stock market, why would I need to sell my system to other people at a seminar? Why not just keep making money for yourself and become a billionaire?"

I did ask that question at a couple of seminars and this is what I was basically told: "I want to share this so that you and many other individuals can lead better lives. I have all the money I need so now it is your turn to profit."

WHAT?

Le Feng, the patron saint of Chinese altruism, died in 1961. He is renowned in China for his spirit of taking pleasure in helping others and his selfless deeds.

These promoters are not Le Feng's. What they say is all bunk. Don't fall for it.

And besides, if everybody had the secret it could not possibly work anymore. The world would be filled with only rich people.

But at the end of the seminar if you are sitting with a "closer" you will be told that you are going to be a member of the select few who will be using this special system. Everybody else who is not using it will lose their money.

How about flipping houses? In my tax practice I meet two or three people every year who have paid thousands of dollars for learning how to flip a house. Of worse they actually did a house.

None of them have had profits to report.

Flipping houses is hard work. The competition to even get the house on the court house steps is ferocious. And if you get it the cost to fix it up may be more than you think. And that special hard money loan they give you? Yep, fifteen percent or more.

And then you have to sell it. More expenses.

Yes, a few make some quick money once in a while, but most individuals I have seen end up with an overvalued property that may take years to recover their invested cost.

What about day traders? You know the ones who claim to beat the market? I have seen several with million dollar loss carry-forwards on their tax returns ($3.3M being the highest to date).

I once had to pony up over $65,000 to cover my losses in the commodities market. I went flying one Monday morning before the market opened. When I returned to my office four hours later I had dozens of frantic calls from my broker.

When I finally reached him, the daily limits had been triggered so no more sell orders were accepted. This is what he had to say to me:

"Lynn, what makes you think you can outsmart all those guys on Wall Street and their real time computer systems?"

The bottom line is this. Never ever enter a proposition where you have to be in the 49% (or less) who have to prove the other 51% (or more) wrong.

That is what day trading and proprietary stock systems must do.

It is just like when your friends go to Las Vegas (or Atlantic City). They always come home and say they won, don't' they.

Do you really think all those gigantic ritzy hotels and casinos were built on the backs of winners?

The right pathway

The pathway to success is to advance in your working career with promotions and to pay yourself first while using those tax breaks that make sense.

Remember the adage, "If it sounds too good to be true, it is!"

There are no saints out there who want to make you rich. The seminar or story or system they are pushing is designed to make them rich.

Period. Dot. End of story.

"I would say you have an ethical obligation to pay the taxes that you owe, but you don't have an ethical obligation to pay taxes that you don't owe. In fact, you should be seeking ways to legally minimize your taxes.

John Mackey (1953 -)

Chapter 7: Tax advantaged investment strategies that actually work

In my original 1984 edition I offered a three step strategy to attain wealth. The three steps were:

Step 1: IRA

Step 2: Own your home

Step 3: Invest accumulated cash

I see no reason to change this strategy in general; rather, I am simply going to modify it based on today's tax code and expand it into a more detailed five step plan.

This five step plan to accomplish financial freedom for you and your family will be finalized in Part 5. Taken together, these five steps will become your investment strategy to follow for the remainder of your working career.

Your final outcome will vary based on your income level (taking into consideration your tax bracket) and the long-term benefits you may have from your employment besides a 401(k) plan.

<u>What you may already have</u>

Briefly, many people below the senior executive level in today's corporate economy have the opportunity to participate in an employee stock purchase plan (ESPP).

These plans allow you to put aside a specified dollar amount of your salary and every six months, based on total participation within your company, buy shares at 85% of the fair market value.

You can then either sell them later; or hold them as long as you want.

Some of you will also have the opportunity to receive stock options from your employer. These are more complex as they have a "strike" price set at the grant date (your purchase price), a "vesting" period before you can exercise them (buy), and an "expiration" date by which time you must either exercise them or lose them.

In addition, they create phantom income (a non-cash taxable fringe benefit) based on the fair market value in excess of the strike price at the time you exercise them.

These plans are important to use; and both take funding. Their cost will simply fall under where you invest your accumulated cash from paying yourself first. Both of these plans are a great way to provide equity positions in your investment portfolio.

I am not covering how these types of plans work beyond my short comments above, as that would almost be a book unto itself.

Suffice it to say, if offered by your company, take them. Unfortunately, over the years as a tax professional I have witnessed the majority of lower income employees simply cash in their shares when eligible and just spend the money.

PLEASE don't do that unless you have no faith in your company. If you feel you must cash them in at least put the money to work somewhere else in your financial portfolio.

Using the Internal Revenue Code (IRC) to build wealth

Having said the above I now return to the three fundamental tax advantages outlined in the early part of this book.

It is upon those tax benefits that a career working individual will build his or her financial portfolio. The tax advantages can work alone or in concert.

You will also incorporate tax preferences as they too play an important part in this strategy.

The remainder of this chapter will deal with these opportunities and explain how each one of them is used to assist you in accumulating wealth. They are as follows:

1. Deductible contributions providing tax savings on a current basis and deferred taxation of earnings:
   a. Company sponsored 401K's
   b. Traditional IRA's
   c. Rental real estate
2. Deferred taxation on capital gains:
   a. The stock market
   b. Real estate both personal and rental
3. Deferred taxation on current earnings and future tax free income:
   a. Roth IRA's
   b. Ordinary annuities
   c. Life insurance cash value

Let's take a look at each of these tax advantages in detail.

Deductible contributions providing tax savings on a current basis and deferred taxation of earnings:

Company sponsored 401(k) retirement plans

There are a number of pension plans in the tax code and they all fall under IRC Section 401(a). Employers have a lot of leeway in the way they are set up but they all work the same tax wise.

Contributions, either from your paycheck, or directly from your employer, or from both, are paid to a trustee for your benefit. These contributions are deducted from your income or your employer's income. They are not taxed. Thus they achieve a primary tax advantage of saving taxes up front.

The names given to these plans are short-hand for the section of the IRC they appear in. The three most prominent general business employee groups are named as:

(1) 401(k) plans for "for profit" organizations;

(2) 403(b) plans for "not for profit" organizations; and

(3) 457(b) plans for "governmental" organizations, for example, city, state, federal and school district employees.

In addition, small businesses may use SIMPLE IRA plans or profit sharing money purchase plans. These plans typically do not allow you to contribute your own money.

My discussion for company sponsored pension plans will simply focus on the term 401(k) as an all-inclusive term since the vast majority of employees have that in today's economy.

If your company provides you with a non-contributory traditional pension plan, wonderful. But realize those contributions are essentially a salary offset being done without any control from you.

Company/government sponsored traditional pension plans are like Social Security (you may have noticed I have made no comment so far about Social Security), as either one is a plan over which you have essentially no control beyond years of service and salary compensation. I do not count them in the pay yourself first concept.

Having said this, my recommendation is that you always use your 401(k) plan to make a contribution to the extent that your employer matches your contribution.

Any contributions that exceed that amount is only from excess discretionary income. I firmly believe you are better off using your additional contribution dollars for other tax advantages that are afforded to you. If you contribute more than the minimum amount to obtain your employer's match, you may deny yourself using a host of other investment options.

I base this on the analysis I did earlier in Chapter 6 when I compared the net tax outcome of a Traditional IRA against a Roth IRA. You will find in your early years you will have far better uses for your savings cash flow for other investment options than simply putting it in your 401(k).

The only time I will concede putting more into your 401(k) is if you are in a high tax bracket during your working years and truly will be in a lower tax bracket in retirement.

Once more allow me to be clear. I am all for using your 401(k) but only to the extent of gaining all of your employer's matching contribution. Your employer's match is "free" money. I don't care if you have to reduce your standard of living; or amend your budget; or simply do without; but...

GET THE FREE MATCHING MONEY FROM YOUR EMPLOYER IN YOUR 401(k).

This is one of the few times in your life that additional money is yours for the taking -- legally. If you do not take advantage of that offer you are missing the boat. Got it?

<u>Traditional Individual Retirement Accounts</u>

The Traditional IRA was created in 1974 with the passage of the Employee Retirement Income Security Act (ERISA). It gave individuals who did not have any form of retirement plan the option to contribute up to $1,500 into a trust that was held by a bank, stock broker or other authorized fiduciary.

It was considered a major breakthrough in providing equality to individuals outside of corporate sponsored pension plans.

In 1981, when President Reagan passed the Economic Recovery Tax Act (ERTA), it ended the limitation that you must not have an employer sponsored retirement plan so that anyone could now contribute up to $2,000. Plus a non-working spouse could contribute to a separate IRA up to $250.

It was on this basis that I established an IRA as the first step in my original investment strategy noted at the beginning of this chapter.

But congress decided this was too much of a giveaway to individuals in higher income tax brackets, so in the 1986 tax reform income restrictions were added and these restrictions remain in the IRC to this day.

In 2018 your ability to contribute begins to phase out for a Traditional IRA at $63,000 if you are single, for married with one spouse covered in a company plan at $189,000, and if both spouses are covered at $101,000.

For a Roth IRA your ability to contribute begins to phase out at $120,000 for single and $189,000 for married filing jointly.

All these restrictions and phase outs are complex and based on MAGI (Modified Adjusted Gross Income. MAGI is your Adjusted Gross Income with a s list of tax preference items of income such as Student Loan Interest, Traditional IRA contributions, and others added back in. To compute MAGI you should consult with a tax professional.

For the vast majority of individuals who are reading this book, your MAGI is probably under these limits and you can contribute to either one. Also you cannot exceed the individual total contribution limit of $5,500 in 2018, as all contributions are combined for both types of IRAs. (Note: there is an added $1,000 catch up allowance if you are over age 50.)

Lastly, even if only one spouse has earned income both spouses may have an IRA and make the maximum contribution allowed.

In my original book I shared I was in the air force in 1974 and, of course, had a non-contributory government funded retirement plan. I had no control over it other than time in service and rank. As a result, I could not have an IRA.

When I wrote Pay Yourself First in 1984, the Individual Retirement Account (IRA) contribution limit was $2,000 and the rules were changed so that anyone could use it. IRA's became a critical way to use tax savings to help fund my financial future.

To understand why I have changed my attitude about the Traditional IRA you need to understand the history of the Roth IRA.

The Roth IRA was created in 1997 with the passage of the Taxpayer Relief Act of 1997 and named for its chief sponsor Senator William Roth of Delaware.

I have detailed the difference between the Traditional and Roth IRA's in Chapter 6. In my opinion the Roth IRA is the single most important part of your investment portfolio. And Senator Roth agreed.

Before he died in 2003, he said, "…if you work hard and save hard, you can have a good retirement income that allows you to leave something to your children."

It is said that he did not quite know what had been created by the IRA that bears his name but it has become one of the most important parts of many Americans' retirement.

This is because of the liberal treatment afforded to a taxpayer after age 59 ½. All withdrawals are tax free, and there is no required minimum distribution at age 70 ½ as in all other retirement plans.

And if you do not take the money out at all (or leave any part of it) you can pass those funds on to your heirs. It is tax free to them.

Facts about the usage of IRA's are hard to find, but after gleaning many sources it is sad for me to say that only eleven percent of all Americans have them as direct accounts (many have them as rollover accounts from a 401(k) when they retire) and of the ones who have IRAs, only a quarter of them contribute on an annual basis.

I consider the Roth IRA to be one of the biggest tax giveaways from congress to individuals in the history of the tax code. And so do some members of congress who now see only higher income individuals using them.

Some efforts have been made in congress to rein them in; but the majority of congress has not given much attention to them.

So my only question is: "What will you do?"

Rental real estate

Owning single family homes and holding them out for rent is still a major source of wealth and future income. But it has some aspects that require serious consideration.

First, if you own one rental you are a landlord. I learned that in 1980. If you think you want to manage a property let me warn you in advance – it is not for the weak of heart.

Calls about plumbing at 2 a.m. or air-conditioning problems as you are about to leave for the weekend are rarely greeted with delight.

Rule #1: Hire a manager. The cost may appear high but the relief from handling tenants, vacancies, and evictions is priceless.

Second, most people enter the rental real estate market when they are either transferred and keep the house they are leaving, or when they move up in size and/or quality to their next home.

If your starter home was at or below the median price for where you live it is a very good candidate to retain as a rental. If it was in the upper cost range it is not.

Rule #2: Don't look at what you would live in; look at what an average income family would live in.

About sixty percent of Americans are already homeowners. The remainder either does not want to own or are not financially qualified to obtain a mortgage. They may be in a career where they are transferred often or simply can't afford the cost of keeping a house properly maintained.

You will be renting to individuals who are sometimes not able to pay you very month; or who do not keep the house as clean as you would. Obey Rule #1 and these concerns melt away.

Third, you must consider the income to capital ratio. In other words what percentage of the value of the property will the annual rent be? That is called the "cap rate" in real estate. Years ago it was 8-10%. Today it is more like 6-7% due to lower mortgage interest costs.

Rule #3: Location. Is the area where your rental home is located going to appreciate in value, stagnate, or drop?

Fourth, what is your modified adjusted gross income? As of 2017, if your MAGI (defined earlier) exceeds $100,000 the deduction for rental income losses begins to phase out so that by $150,000 MAGI you can no longer deduct any loss. However, un-allowed loss deductions are carried forward to when you sell the property and then you get that benefit no matter your income.

Additionally, the total rental loss write-off if you are under the stated MAGI levels is limited to $25,000. That is a hefty write-off if you are single and in the 22% or 24% bracket; or married and in the 22% tax bracket.

Rule #4: Is the benefit worth the time?

In today's market a condo is the best of all rentals. It has a very high cap rate and is usually already in a position for a manager. I recommend holding onto condos.

For a single family home ask these questions. Is it in an acceptable neighborhood? Does it have appreciation value? Will you have any tax benefits?

Remember Rule #3. What is a good location today may not be so in twenty to thirty years.

Use common sense, and as the song by Kenny Rogers in 1978 went, "…you got to know when to hold'em, know when to fold'em…"

Fifth, the outright purchase of rental real estate properties is a very competitive market. Don't go for the flip that house concept, it does not work. If you want to invest in where you live, and do some sweat equity, great.

Rule #5: Invest in rental real estate for the long haul.

In the long run it is appreciation that will be your primary investment return followed by positive cash flow in retirement, your best benefit of all. Why? Because somebody else paid off the mortgage and now the cash is flowing in..

Deferred taxation on capital gains

This is a tax preference item only. It simply means that no tax is due on the gain of a capital asset, whether held for investment or personal use, until it is sold; and then only if it has a gain. Deferral is not a tax advantage unto itself.

Deferral becomes a tax advantage only if, at the time of sale, it has a lower tax bracket than your ordinary income tax bracket. This is called the Long Term Capital Gains rate (LTCG). To achieve LTCG you must hold a capital asset for a specified time period, currently more than one year.

For 2016 and 2017 the maximum long-term capital gains tax rate was twenty percent (20%). It had been fifteen percent (15%) for a number of years in the past; and higher for some other years before that (28% in 1986).

Beginning in 2018, under the 2017 Tax Cuts and Jobs Act, long term capital gains (LTCG) rates are based on your filing status and your <u>taxable</u> income ranges as follows:

Long-Term Capital Gains Rate	Single	Married Filing Jointly	Head of House hold	Married Filing Separately
0%	$0 to $38,700	$0 to $77,400	$0 to $51,850	$0 to $38,700
15%	$38,701 to $426,700	$77,401 to $480,050	$51,851 to $453,350	$38,701 to $240,025
20%	$426,701 or more	$480,051 or more	$453,351 or more	$240,026 or more

The stock market

Whether held as individual shares of stock, either in a brokerage account or a certificate in your safety deposit box, no tax is due until you sell those shares and only if sold at a gain.

Mutual fund shares are also treated the same with one exception. If the fund makes any internal sales during the year and they have gains, those gains are passed through to you as a taxable event even if you do not receive any cash.

Most investors in mutual funds allow the manager to reinvest the proceeds from internal sales and simply report the gains on their individual tax returns.

If you need cash to pay the taxes, perhaps on a large holding, you would need to either ask the fund to distribute the cash to you, or sell some shares to cover the tax which may trigger even more gains subject to taxation.

Lastly, the mutual fund manager will identify the internal sales as long-term gains for tax purposes.

No matter how you hold stock, any dividends, whether paid to you in cash, reinvested inside the mutual fund, or used to buy additional stock shares through a dividend re-investment plan, are all taxable as dividend income whether received in cash or not.

Further, under current law, if they are qualified dividends (that generally means a U.S. based corporation) they are taxed under the LTCG tax rate. This is a great tax benefit as from 1954 to 2003 they were taxed as ordinary income at the taxpayers full income tax rate.

Beginning in 2003, qualified dividends became subject to the LTCG tax rate which was 15% until 2015. In 2016 it was raised to 20% or your tax bracket whichever was lower. And for the lowest tax bracket they were exempt from taxation.

As you have seen on the chart showing the LTCG rates on the previous page, beginning in 2018, for the vast majority of taxpayers they will be either no tax or a 15% tax rate.

<u>Real estate</u>

One of the great beauties of owning real estate is appreciation. This applies to rental property, investment in raw land, and your own home.

Long and short, the deferral of taxation is a major factor in owning real estate. You want it to go up in value and you don't have to sell it unless you want. And, if you do sell it after holding it a long time, it should be taxed at a lower long-term capital gains tax rate

Of course congress tinkers with these factors from time to time, but over history capital assets held for a long time have always had some form of tax preference or tax advantage.

Use common sense. Educate yourself or seek out a trusted tax advisory to guide you.

So, in conclusion, this second section has outlined the underlying fundamental basis for building and protecting long-term wealth.

<u>Deferred taxation on current earnings and future tax free income</u>

This third section on the three fundamental tax advantages ties together the most important of all combinations.

If you can defer taxation on current earnings, and then take out the proceeds income tax free, that is probably the single best combination.

In the first section I addressed deductible contributions or investments, but in each case when the money came out at retirement it was fully taxed.

Even the once generous money machine of rental real estate created in 1981 has been curbed by follow-on tax law changes.

In the end, only you can determine which one worked the best and that involves the complex system of present value analysis.

But a sound investment portfolio will hold all types of assets and each one for different reasons. I will pull all of this together in Part 5, but for the moment, allow me to address the three types of assets you may not have given much consideration to until you read this book.

Roth IRA's

Anyone who qualifies for a contribution to a Roth IRA and does not do so is missing the boat or train or whatever metaphor you like.

If your income allows you to fund a Roth IRA and put the funds into the stock market, do so. You get tax deferral on the gains and when you take the money out in retirement it is tax free.

I proved the value of the Roth over the Traditional IRA (and that includes the 401(k) too) in Chapter 6.

I also emphasized to only contribute the amount of money into your 401(k) that is required to obtain your employer's matching money earlier in this chapter.

Having said this, there is no discussion left. USE YOUR ROTH IRA if you are qualified by your income level and you will not regret it later.

Annuities

Annuities are a very poorly understood product.

First off they are "sold" by life insurance companies, and as your mom and dad taught you, you are to avoid life insurance agents at all costs (laughter included).

Secondly annuities have more than one option. In the past an annuity was simply an exchange of a sum of money with a life insurance company for the promise to pay a specific amount (the annuity) to you (or your surviving spouse) for the remainder of your (and his or her) life.

A standard annuity contract provides guaranteed income that you can not outlive. It is an excellent adjunct to Social Security. Both payments last for your lifetime.

So what are the options I mentioned? To understand you have to first determine where the funds came from. Were they "out of pocket" after tax dollars; or were they a rollover of an IRA or 401(k)?

If the funds are out of your pocket, then it is like a combination of the Traditional/Roth IRA. You do not have to take any money until you want (this is called a deferred annuity) or you can begin an immediate payment (called an immediate annuity).

Whenever you do take money out you are only taxed on the portion of each distribution that is earnings. Think of a standard annuity as an account where you can dip in when you want; or you can annuitize it at any time into a guaranteed lifetime income.

When you annuitize to a lifetime income, the rate of return at the time is very important. If interest is low your payment will be less than when interest is high. As a result, at the present time, out of pocket annuities are not that popular.

Now, if the funds come from a tax-deferred fund like an IRA/401(k), a similar set of rules apply just as if it were still in your IRA/401(k). You must take money out beginning at age 70 ½ and the insurance carrier will compute that for you. You may take more; but one aspect is that annuities usually have penalties if you want the money back too soon.

You may have a straight annuity invested in the general fund of the insurance carrier or it can be in the stock market. Annuities are complex. So consider every aspect when you evaluate an annuity.

One big tax exception that may lead you in retirement to consider an annuity is long term care. If you become unable to care for yourself, and you have money in an IRA/401(k) and withdraw it, it is taxed.

Conversely, if those funds are in a tax-qualified annuity and the monthly payment goes directly to a long-term care facility, that distribution is not taxed. This even applies to some non-tax qualified annuities.

This is a great benefit to have if you should require such care as over half of all individuals will need some form of long term care at some point in their life.

In conclusion, if you reach a point in life with a large IRA or 401(k) fund and are headed to long term care, consult a trusted insurance agent who understands the options. They are complex and beyond the scope of this book, but the tax benefits can be awesome.

Life Insurance

Why am I including "life insurance" in my list of potential investments?

First, nearly every person needs life insurance. We know it should really be called death insurance but it would be hard to sell with that title. This is a "truth" about life.

As a statistical matter only two percent of all Americans die by age twenty-five. After a person reaches age 25 about fifteen percent of them will die before they attain age sixty-five. If you are forty, twelve percent of you will die by age sixty-five.

The reality is if you are married and have a family you need life insurance. (Note: an abbreviated life expectancy table is provided in Chapter 9.)

Second, and more important, life insurance can be a very attractive part of an investment portfolio based on how it is designed and used by the person who owns it, especially if based upon that person's needs for death benefit coverage. This is also a "truth."

Having declared these two truths let's begin with the following question. What is life insurance?

Webster's dictionary provides twenty definitions of "life" but only these two apply:

1 a: the quality that distinguishes a vital and functional being from a dead body

5 a: the period from birth to death

For my purposes that means a living person -- YOU.

Webster's provides two definitions of "insurance" but only one applies:

1 a: the business of insuring persons or property

b: coverage by contract whereby one party undertakes to indemnify or guarantee another against loss by a specified contingency or peril

c: the sum for which something is insured

All insurance is a contract between the insured and the insuring party, usually a regulated insurance company. The agreement provides for you to pay a premium in exchange for the insurance company to pay you for the loss / damage to the insured item.

For example, auto insurance pays for repairs in the event you damage your car; theft insurance pays for the cost or value of the item stolen; fire insurance pays for damage to a building or personal property from fire; health insurance pays medical bills when you are sick. Having said this let's examine life insurance.

I began this section with the question: "Why am I including life insurance in my list of potential investments?"

I then gave you two answers that I called truths; unfortunately, most likely you have only heard negative comments such as:

- "Life insurance is a bad investment."
- "Life insurance only pays if I die and then why do I care."
- "Life insurance costs too much."
- And the best one of all: "I won't die any time soon."

For the average person the amount of life insurance one needs is the amount that if he or she dies his or her spouse can continue with a lifestyle equal to what they had when he or she was alive.

And for those of you with children the biggest issue will be is there enough money to care for them and allow them to go to college and reach the dreams you have for them.

So how much coverage does it take? You get to decide, but generally you need an amount equal to your mortgage (or present value of rent), the discounted future value of college expenses when the children reach age eighteen, and enough additional cash to pay all your current bills.

Then add about one-half of the present value of the insured spouse's income and you have an accurate total figure.

And don't forget in a two income family both spouses need to be covered for one-half of the present value of their current income.

When you add it all up it can be a pretty big number. But do you actually need that much for the rest of your life?

NO! You do not need that much for all your life. As you live and earn and save, the total amount of "net death benefit" will continuously be reduced over time.

So how does that work? Once your current need is established, the second truth is achieved by the design of your life insurance portfolio over your lifetime. To accomplish this you need a basic understanding of the three primary types of life insurance which are: (1) Term; (2) Permanent; and (3) Investment Based.

Term is easy. Many of you already have it at work as part of your employer's fringe benefit package called "group term life insurance."

The down side of group insurance is it usually ends when you leave that company (you can buy it out but it is usually very expensive) and/or your next employer may not offer as much or none at all.

A personal Term policy has two parts. First is the payment of a premium; and second is a fixed death benefit only (no cash value).

Most term is for a stated number of years such as 10, 15, 20, 25, or even 30 years. It can have either a level premium or an annual renewable premium that starts low but goes up each year.

In every case at the end of the term of years the premium goes up so much only very very ill people who expect to die soon even consider keeping Term.

Term is generally inexpensive if you are young and healthy and do not need it past about the age of fifty-five. Does Term sound like a product that would protect you and your spouse against either one's death during the child rearing years? Yes it does.

Permanent is typically whole life or guaranteed universal life. You plan to keep it until you die. It is used by many individuals who want to leave an estate to cover final expenses or cover potential nursing home expenses.

What -- nursing home expenses? Yes! Today's permanent types of life insurance allow the insured to withdraw an annual amount (usually not to exceed 24% of the face value) per year up to 96% of the face value IF you are confined to a nursing home and meet the listed criteria of being unable to care for yourself.

As a result modern day life insurance has virtually eliminated the need to purchase long-term care insurance.

Investment Based life insurance is where I want to focus your attention. There are two parts of special permanent life insurance policies that will accomplish two objectives at once for you.

The first part is to provide a death benefit, just like term, called the "net amount at risk" within the policy.

The second part is the cash value inside the policy that can become a major investment asset depending on the structure of the policy and the premiums paid into the policy.

Why this works is the three fundamental tax advantages of all life insurance.

First, and the most important, under the U.S. tax code the death benefits paid by a life insurance policy are totally free of income taxes.

Second, during the accumulation period of a cash value policy, any gain from earnings in excess of the total premiums paid is tax-deferred, and then tax-free at death.

Third, you may withdraw your basis in the policy at some future point tax-free. There are lots of rules for this third and last tax condition and I will leave it to an agent to explain but suffice it to say you may access the total of the premiums you paid into the policy over your lifetime (your basis) any time you want during your retirement years.

It is the management of the second and third features noted above that makes an Investment Based life insurance policy a very attractive part of your overall lifetime investment and savings portfolio.

And all the while the policy is covering your family's needs for cash in the event of your or your spouse's premature death.

A final method to take money out of a life insurance policy tax free is to borrow against your cash value. You then have the potential of ever growing interest payments to keep the policy in force; and this strategy is best left until you are much older and expect to die before using up all of the cash value.

Then at your death the loan is paid off tax free.

But if you outlive the loan (run out of cash value) the policy could lapse and the money withdrawn would become taxable or you would have to pay potentially very large premiums back into the policy to prevent it from lapsing.

You have to carefully plan and manage this last option.

How life insurance works as an investment

There are really only two types of policies to consider as an Investment Based product. One is called Variable Universal Life (VUL); and the other is called Indexed Universal Life (IUL).

Variable Universal Life is a registered security product and the selling agent must hold a securities license.

In the VUL product, the cash value is invested in a family of mutual funds or bond funds just like those explained earlier in the section on the stock market. You, the owner of the policy, determine the funds to invest your premium payments and you have the option to move between fund accounts if you wish.

Essentially you have a mutual fund wrapped inside a universal life insurance policy that provides long-term tax deferred growth.

Contrast this to directly owning a mutual fund where you pay annual taxes on the dividends and internal sales of stocks, thus lowering your overall return.

In the IUL product the cash value is indexed against an established stock index like the S&P 500 or the Dow Jones Industrials. Your cash value goes up as these indexes move up.

A distinct advantage of the IUL product over the VUL product is that if the stock market goes down, your IUL cash value does not go down. The IUL account is guaranteed to never go down. As a result the upside may not be as high as inside the VUL.

There are many variables in these products including cost issues and other rules so you need an agent you can trust to fully explain them so you can understand what you are buying.

To use either of these products as part of for your investment portfolio you must pay a premium much larger than the minimum required to fund the death benefit's cost within the policy.

In other words, your goal over the years is for the policy to become more and more cash value and less and less death benefit (called net amount at risk).

As a result, two things are happening inside an Investment Based life insurance policy. First, the term insurance cost (based on the "net amount at risk") is being funded with pre-tax dollars. This is because the cost of insurance is deducted from the earnings inside the policy.

In contrast a Term policy's premiums come from your after-tax income.

Second, as the cash value grows the net amount at risk is being reduced so that you are buying less and less life insurance over time thus controlling your cost of insurance over your working career.

An Investment Based life policy is a win-win for those dollars allocated in your investment plan to support your need for life insurance and, at the same time, accumulate wealth over your working career.

I have illustrations on the next couple of pages to graphically illustrate how term and investment based policies work. If you need to learn more search the internet and study these types of policies; then contact a life insurance agent you trust to learn more until you are ready to move forward,

When you pay yourself first you can place extra money into the policies on a regular basis over your investing years and that extra money is then invested inside the policy as free cash reserves and not used to fund the death benefit.

WARNING: you need to be fairly healthy for this strategy to work and you need to have excess cash flow.

The three types of life insurance policies in picture format follow.

Term Life Policy $250,000 face value, Male age 30 non-tobacco preferred health with 20-year level pay premium of $205.

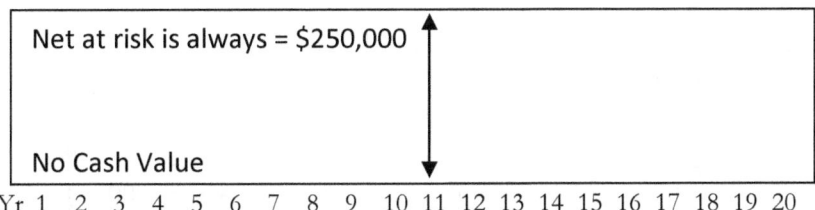

Total Premiums Paid equal over 20 yrs are $4,100 and policy then converts to Annual Renewable Term (ART). The ART premium for year 21 is $1,725, by year 30 it's $4,115, and by year 40 it's $11,060.

If the above male is still healthy he could apply again. For example, he could obtain the same policy for another 20 years for a level premium of $590 a year. Then at age 71 the premium jumps to $12,115. By age 80, life expectancy, this individual would have paid in a total of $250,000 for both series of term policies.

But remember, eventually no one keeps term unless they are really sick; but it should be a vital part of an individual's life insurance plan in the early years especially if disposable income is tight.

Universal life comes in two options. The first is called <u>level</u> where the death benefit payable remains the same over the life of the contract. As you internally accrue cash value the net amount at risk to the insurance company declines; thus, the internal cost of insurance (COI) is being paid on a lower risk of death amount.

Just like term insurance, as the policy owner ages, the annual cost of insurance goes up inside the policy. By using a level policy as part of an insurance plan it can contain that cost as premiums over the minimum accumulate and offset part of the net at risk.

Variable Universal Life Policy $250,000 face value, Male age 30, non-tobacco with <u>level</u> death benefit of $250,000 and annual premium of $1,200.

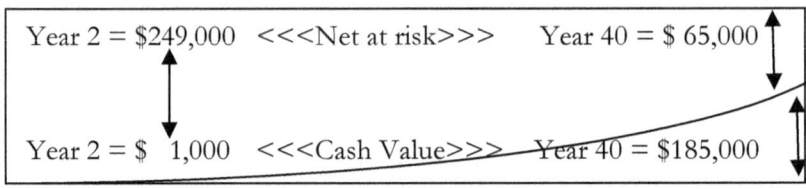

Year 2 = $249,000 <<<Net at risk>>>   Year 40 = $ 65,000

Year 2 = $ 1,000 <<<Cash Value>>>   Year 40 = $185,000

Yr 2   4   6   8   10 12 14 16 18 20 22 24 26 28 30 32 34 36 38 40

Total Premiums Paid over 40 yrs equals $48,000; and if the policy earns a net return of 6% after the cost of insurance the future cash value at age 60 will be approximately $185,000.

The second option for universal life is called <u>increasing</u>. This means that the death benefit payable is the initial face amount of the policy PLUS any cash value. If the insured dies the total benefit check is more than a level policy by the amount of the cash value. The following chart will illustrate this.

Variable Universal Life Policy $250,000 face value, Male age 30 non-tobacco with <u>increasing</u> death benefit of $250,000 and annual premium of $1,500 a year.

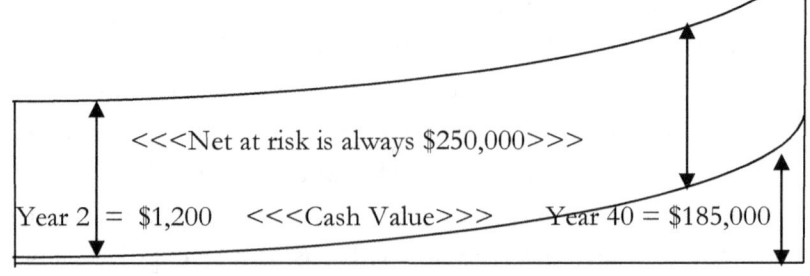

<<<Net at risk is always $250,000>>>

Year 2 = $1,200   <<<Cash Value>>>   Year 40 = $185,000

Yr   2 4   6   8   10 12 14 16 18 20 22 24 26 28 30 32 34 36 38 40

Total Premiums Paid over 40 yrs equals $60,000; and if the policy earns a net return of 6% after the cost of insurance the future cash value at age 60 will be approximately $185,000. If death occurs the payment is $250,000 PLUS the cash value on the date of death. For example, if death occurred in year 40, the payment to your heirs would be $435,000 ($250,000 net at risk plus $185,000 cash value).

You will have noticed in the above two charts that the premium required to create the same future cash value was twenty-five percent more for the <u>increasing</u> policy over the <u>level</u> policy ($1,500 per year versus $1,200). That is due to the constantly growing cost of the total net insurance at risk (constant in one; shrinking in the other).

The selection of which type to use or even use one of each depends on your total life insurance needs. As a primary Investment Based policy the level type is usually best. Conversely, the increasing type can be considered to be "buy term and invest the difference."

If you can afford the cash flow use the increasing type over your working years so that as you add extra money the net coverage protecting your family does not decrease.

Said another way, suppose you were to drop some extra cash into a level policy and then die shortly thereafter. Your family will receive the same amount they would have received the day before you added the cash (the level face value of the policy).

On the day after they don't get the cash you deposited into the policy as it is included in the level face value; while on the day before you added the cash they would get that cash and the policy's face value.

Conversely, with the increasing policy if you add extra cash and then die shortly after that your family gets that cash back in addition to the face value of the policy.

One significant consideration about the increasing type of policy is that when you retire you have the right to convert an increasing policy to a level paid-up policy thus significantly reducing the internal cost of insurance. If you are able to meet with a trusted agent he or she can explain this.

I am an advocate of life insurance. I have orphans in my extended family that were able to go to college and attain the goals of their parents who both died when they were small.

You need to understand life insurance. Be careful to avoid agents who simply want to get a sale made, especially if the proposed product is only whole life. That is the highest commission; not the highest value for the cash.

Whole life works over the long term, but when you are young and short of disposable income a mix of term with level/increasing universal life is probably the optimal way to get the most coverage.

Remember, family need drives life insurance; but long-term growth of cash value in a properly structured mix of life insurance can be a very valuable part of your long-term investment strategy.

This will be further detailed in Part 5.

"Every man is the architect of his own fortune."

- Gaius Sallustius Crispus (86 - 34 B.C.)

Part 5
Your Strategy to Future Wealth

Before I outline the strategy for you to use to attain future wealth and financial freedom, a quick review of the three secrets is in order.

In addition, I will elaborate on the two essential investment types of assets that have proven to reward investors over the past sixty years or more in America.

Using the Three Secrets

Part 1: "The First Secret" began with the following statement:

"The single greatest asset the vast majority of us will ever have in our lifetime is our individual earning power from our chosen profession, talent, or skill."

And from that beginning you now have all three secrets that allow an American with an income to attain future wealth.

But you must have the discipline to use these secrets and over time be able to adapt them as needed when, not if, tax laws and economic environments change.

Change is a constant law of the universe. Our life on earth is but a short interval in that cosmic cycle. Use your lifetime of income well. You only get to do so once.

Obviously, nothing happens until you <u>Pay Yourself First</u>. If you do not use the first secret, no matter what your income level, you will never become wealthy.

I have previously outlined the basics of how to pay yourself first. It begins with a separate checking account into which you deposit an amount from every paycheck.

Now I understand being financial challenged. If you are living "paycheck to paycheck" you may think this is impossible to do. But it is not.

Start your special checking account with as little as one percent (1%) of your paycheck. I know you can do that. If you can do more, do so. If it hurts a little bit, that's OK.

If you have to find the money cut back on eating out each month, or go to less costly locations. There is always somewhere in your spending that can be reduced. Wherever you find it the result will be allowing you to begin paying yourself first.

One other strategy to increase the amount you pay yourself is when you finally pay off your car loan don't buy another one!

Instead, keep making the same payment but into your investment account. It will become a reserve for potential repairs as well be earning money versus becoming more depreciation.

Give that idea some thought.

Part 2: "The Second Secret" began by saying, "…compound interest was the Eighth Wonder of the World"

Having said that what assets will provide you with the best returns to achieve future wealth? And what expectation of rates of return will you be able to achieve to accomplish that?

In my opinion, after forty-five years of experience, the two winners for your investing future are the stock market and rental real estate.

Part 3: "The Third Secret" was <u>How the Tax Code Helps You Grow Wealth</u>.

In that part I outlined how to use tax advantages and tax preferences to help increase your profit; or shield your risk.

To quote from the first edition of this book,

> "Why would Uncle Sam help you out? The answer is that the basic economic principle in the United States, as in most of the Western world today, is capitalism. No other nation has refined this to the point that the United States has. Maybe because we are the youngest of the capitalistic countries, or maybe because we have had such an ardent romance with individualism during our industrial boom. At any rate, the fact is that our economic system is structured by our tax code."

I no longer believe that risk is its own reward. The tax code today does not provide enough current write-offs for losses to offset undo risk (like it did when tax rates were 50% on earned income).

And besides, most people using this strategy are not in the highest tax brackets. The vast majority will be in the mid-brackets and lower brackets. Thus the risk offset is not worth it.

We grow old slowly; you should also get rich slowly.

And the fast buck plans I mentioned earlier virtually always benefit only the promoters.

"If it was easy everyone would do it."

- Lynn O. High (1944 -)

Chapter 8: Two winners for your investing future

It has been said that real estate has made more millionaires than any other method in America.

Maybe, but so has the stock market, especially over the long haul.

Let's examine the stock market first. Here are some data for you to consider about the stock market.

Using the S&P 500, from its beginning in 1928 to 2014, its total rate of return has been ten percent (10%) per year.

For the recent past, from 1950 to 2010 the S&P hit seven percent (7%) right on the head. Recall in the charts I have shown in previous chapters for future outcomes that I used 7% as my rate of return for analysis.

To paraphrase a recent quote from Warren Buffet, "…including dividends six to seven percent (6-7%) is a good number to use for future long term market returns."

But as in anything, nothing is assured and all you and I can do is position ourselves for the best potential outcome.

It is important to understand that this figure includes the reinvestment of all dividends. As a general rule you have a choice on index mutual funds on what to do with the dividends. Reinvest into the same fund, or pay them to you in cash and put them into your accumulation account..

Actual mutual funds will not earn the full index yield due to internal fees and costs. In a no-load mutual fund (and nearly all good ones today do not rely on a sales force so they do not have direct commissions) the cost is called a 12b-1 fee and limited to 0.25% of the assets.

If they are marketed through brokers and other managers, the 12b-1 fee is higher but by SEC regulation cannot exceed 1%.

Read the fund's prospectus carefully to understand what these charges entail and compare different fund expense ratios.

Lastly, there are over 9,000 mutual funds in the United States. So many that it almost becomes impossible for the average person to evaluate one from another.

Consider this, there are just under 3,000 stocks listed on the New York Stock Exchange and just over 3,000 listed on the NASDAQ.

There are more mutual funds than stocks! Working through the thousands of mutual funds is virtually impossible. Most investors use a family of funds (of which there are several hundred) for several reasons.

First, you can move money between different funds without sales fees. This is a big advantage that allows you to balance between sectors and individual fund objectives over time.

Second, a company called Morningstar provides basic information to the general public for your analysis of each family of funds. This is useful in evaluation of both performance and cost over time. (Note: you may also pay a nominal monthly fee to subscribe to additional services with Morningstar.)

Third, you will have the opportunity to use several different family funds over time and compare directly within your own accounts (401(k), Roth IRA, and Variable Universal Life).

Remember, you and I are little fish in a very big pond. Neither you nor I can alter the course of the market by our actions. We are usually just along for the ride.

Having said that I strongly urge you to not try and time the market. Most people, including myself, have failed miserably doing that. The only consideration is sector rebalancing. If you want to engage in that, read about it, study it and then use it sparingly.

I strongly recommend that you only use high quality large mutual fund families (you can figure out who they are for yourself) but there are only about a dozen.

And within each family of funds I recommend that you stick to one or two growth funds, one large-cap fund, an S&P 500 index fund, and a small amount in an income fund.

Over time the income fund will increase its allocation as you grow into retirement. The mix is yours to decide.

There are hundreds of books on the stock market and you have many years to learn. I recommend you read a good number of them and cull out the few tips that may help you manage your investment portfolio. You will need to do this as someday your pay yourself first accounts will grow to impressive values.

Bottom line is this -- stocks will make up the majority, if not nearly all, of your investment assets outside of real estate.

Turning now to real estate, the answer to why it has done well over time is nearly impossible for me, or anyone else, to give. The only three tips I can share are: location, location, and location.

First off, I hope that narrowed it down (laughter included).

I have never owned raw land next to a growing metropolis but there are families who have became very wealthy when a major city ran over their family farm.

As for me, I had farm land in the middle of nowhere. Having grandpa's farm go up 1000% over time as a big city grew nearby never happened.

Secondly, most of us will never be involved in owning large-scale commercial real estate. In the past twenty years the rate of return on high quality commercial properties has been about ten percent (10%). Over many years it narrows down to more like eight percent (8%).

About the only way for a small investor to enter commercial real estate is through Real Estate Investment Trusts (REITs). Do so at your own analysis and risk tolerance.

For most of us the single family residence is going to be our principal real estate investment. And for that the long-term rate of return has been one percent (1%) plus the inflation rate. The inflation rate is available from the Bureau of Labor Statistics (BLS) using the consumer price index (CPI).

You don't really buy a home to profit. Oh once in a while you will, but then you have to sell it and go live somewhere else. Over time the home you own and live in is NOT an investment. It is a storehouse of value that hopefully will be paid off by retirement.

The greatest value of home ownership is pride of ownership and you can paint the walls any color you want.

Okay, back to real estate. Using 1984 as base 100, as of May, 2016, the CPI is 240. That translates into an annual year over year increase of 4.4. (Note: in CPI analysis one does not compound. It is the annual assessment of the basket of goods and services at that year's price. If you did compound, it you would have a 2.8% rate.)

Since 1950 (to compare with the previous stock market data) to 2010 real estate has had an annual year over year increase of 3.2%.

That is in line with other government statistics in general.

So, add 1% to 2.8% and you get 3.8% as the average annual rate of appreciation for single family homes.

But that alone cannot be used for comparison because of the tax benefits along the way (depreciation) of rental property and of course the rental income to offset expenses. That figure is simply the growth in value of the property itself.

Thus my answer to where you end up on rental real estate is, "I don't know."

I only know that three of the seven rental houses I bought in Las Vegas in 1980 and held until 2001 doubled in value. I had only minor costs along the way and paid off about half the mortgages using other people's rent money.

I sold one other rental house plus a four-plex in 1982 at a small profit; and I gave up two other rental houses in a divorce settlement in 1983.

Conversely, the two houses I bought in 1981 in Hawaii (considered a no lose area) I sold one for what I paid; and the other at a small loss. And I had negative cash flow for both of them.

As far as the seven houses that I have personally owned to live in, one for over fifteen years, the rest for an average of three years, I made a little money on three, a lot on one, lost a little money on two and lost a lot on one.

Scoreboard on home ownership is: 1 win, 1 loss, and 5 draws.

But you (or I) don't buy a personal home to profit. Here's why.

I have a good friend who lives in Las Vegas, Nevada. He returned from overseas in 1985 and bought a very nice big house for $300,000. He retired from the air force a few years later.

In 2006 he was offered $1,300,000 for it. He told me bluntly if he sold it where would he then live? Another house of similar quality but in lesser area would be at least one million. And he didn't want the hassle of moving.

Then the real estate market crashed in Las Vegas in 2007/08 and his house fell in market value to $450,000 having owned it for 22 years.

He didn't care. He liked living in his paid for house on the slopes south of town. The view was great and he didn't care about the home's value. It was his.

I saw him in 2016 and the house was back up to $900,000 in value. And who knows what will happen until he decides to sell perhaps when he is much older.

The moral to this story is your personal home is where you live. Over maybe forty years, and at the right time, maybe you can take a big profit and move on to a retirement home elsewhere for less cost. Operative work is "maybe."

You will need to reduce your upkeep due to age and or health someday. I just bought my retirement home in Phoenix, Arizona, this past month.

I have lived in Dallas, Texas, for the past twenty-four years. Beginning in 2015, people were being transferred to north Texas from California and other places. The folks from California had sold their 1,800 sq ft homes for $1.3M and found they could now buy an 8,000 sq ft home for $1M here in Texas.

Most don't need that large a house, so a nice 4,000 sq ft home with pool at $450K seems a bargain to them. They have been shocked at the low cost of homes in Texas. (We have low cost land but very high property taxes; offset by no state income tax.)

Everything I know about real estate is own it if it falls your way, like keeping that first condo you bought, or your first starter home, and turn them into rentals. Rental real estate can provide an important part of the balance you will need when the rest of your portfolio is all in stocks.

Lastly, I have not addressed bonds. I am not a big proponent of bonds, either in the past or today. The risk of being caught holding bonds that fluctuate in value when interest rates change is best left to the long-term bond experts, such as life and annuity companies.

There may be a place in your retirement portfolio someday for bonds, but for now they have no place in building wealth.

To conclude at this point, you most likely will be relying on the stock market for most of your future appreciation of your investment holdings, along with some real estate.

And the principle tax advantage will be deferral of gains in both taxable and tax-deferred accounts followed by long-term capital gains tax rates when you cash out. When you take money from your Roth IRA or life insurance policy, that money will be tax-free.

Leave gold to the "gold bugs" and oil and gas exploration to the oil barons like T. Boone Pickens and the giant energy corporations like Exxon and Mobil. I have owned a share in over two dozen oil wells and have never made a net dollar. It ain't worth the hassle.

Besides, you will most likely end up holding many positions in energy stocks through a mutual fund aimed that way, or through the large-cap funds that will include shares of the oil giants in their holdings. Be a mini-oil baron that way please.

Remember, your principle and most likely only tax write-off will be your 401(k) contributions. But when you take that money out in retirement it will be fully taxable.

Rental real estate is a great supplement in retirement too.

And finally a Roth IRA account and cash value in life insurance policies gives you tax-free money when you want it.

With the knowledge you have attained at this point in the book and your understandings of taxes, investments and the principle of long-term wealth accumulations, let us not turn to my final chapter: Five Steps to Financial Freedom strategy.

"People used to ask me why I made more money than they did. Simple, I would reply, I am willing to do what other people don't want to do."

- Lynn O. High (1944 -)

Chapter 9: Five Steps to Financial Freedom strategy

The five steps are:
1. 401(k) at work.
2. Roth IRA (if your income allows you to contribute).
3. Investment based life insurance (to the extent your family needs death protection).
4. Own your own home.
5. Rental real estate.

For the vast majority of you reading this book, you will follow these five steps in order using funds set aside from paying yourself first for all but number 4.

Number 4 will simply be a budgeted cost of living; but still an important asset in your overall strategy.

Number 3 is also important, but may be delayed due to your budget. I will address that shortly, but, suffice it to say, when you are newly married and young your life insurance budget may be limited to group term insurance at work and an outside term policy on each other. But as time goes by you must manage life insurance to become a part of your investment portfolio.

STEP ONE: Use your 401(k) plan at work

If you have a 401(k) at work, and your employer offers any matching money, withhold whatever it takes from your paycheck to get that matching money.

It is probably the only free money you will most likely ever receive in your adult lifetime. (I am not saying you won't win the Publishers Clearing House contest, or the lottery, but I doubt either is a reliable way to plan for your retirement.)

Employers have choices for this matching money such as matching up to the first 3% you contribute, or matching half of the first 4-6% you withhold, etc.

I don't care what the formula is you must do this. You avoid federal and state income tax on the money withheld; but not FICA (Social Security and Medicare) and you get free money.

Employers have vesting requirements in order for you to keep the matching money should you leave them too soon. For example, 100% at three years of service or 20% per year for the first five years of service. Vesting only applies to the matching money.

It is important to understand vesting, but vesting should never stop you from making your contribution. That is always your money.

Although a 401(k) is fully taxable when you retire and draw money out, the added future balance from the matching funds more than compensates.

As I commented earlier only put more into your 401(k) if you are in the 28% or higher income tax bracket and you are denied using a Roth IRA.

Additionally, you should fully fund all of your other investment options first and only then, if you still have additional discretionary income, put more into your 401(k).

STEP TWO: Open a Roth IRA

I previously called this the greatest tax give away in the IRC that I have seen in my lifetime (so far). I doubt congress will ever make a better one. And I am pretty sure they will not take this one away. If they did, what you had at that point in time would be grandfathered.

If you qualify based on your income to contribute to a Roth IRA, put the maximum amount into it every year ($5,500 for 2018). You may also do so for both you and your spouse (that's $5,500 each and she does not have to be employed).

Your ability to contribute to a Roth IRA in 2018 begins to phase out at $120,000 for single and $189,000 for married filing jointly.

But the enduring value of the Roth IRA is that you will have an investment account that is tax deferred and converts at age 59 ½ to a tax free asset.

Now, what do you invest your Roth IRA in? I think it is pretty clear from the prior discussion in this Part 5 that the stock market is your only true option.

You may open your Roth IRA with one of the major family of mutual fund companies and self-direct into which funds the money is placed. Over time, then, you become the architect of your own fortune.

Generally, as previously noted, during your younger years growth oriented funds are the most appropriate. When you retire, income funds may become better suited for you. It all depends on your other assets in retirement.

Again, I recommend as you grow in wealth and age you study these issues by reading financial books and other advisories. At retirement you may also choose to move your funds to a managed account with a major brokerage firm, or a private manager for a fee.

It is your money. It is your life. DO NOT fail to use the Roth IRA during your accumulation years ahead of all other holdings.

It is the single best financial method to accumulate tax advantaged wealth that congress has provided to us today.

STEP THREE: Investment based life insurance

In Chapter 7 I stated that there are really only two types of policies to consider as an Investment Based product. One is called Variable Universal Life (VUL) and the other is called Indexed Universal Life (IUL).

This remains true and I am now going to provide you with a blueprint for your life insurance needs. I outlined the best mix of products to cover your needs in a cost effective manner, as well as be a significant part of your financial portfolio.

<u>Needs</u>

The single biggest question most young people have about life insurance is, "How much is enough?"

I don't have an easy answer, but I know an old saying about life insurance: "Widows always complain that the proceeds are too low; insureds always complain that the premiums are too high."

To begin let's have a short talk about insurance. Do you have car insurance? Why. Most people say if they wreck their car they need another one. And they can't afford to buy it without the insurance.

What about fire insurance on your house? Same response.

And of course both the mortgage company and the lender on your car require you to have insurance as well as the state which requires liability insurance on your car.

You see, we all have insurance for two primary reasons: (1) to replace a lost asset; and (2) to cover a tort (law suit) claim if we were responsible for another person's loss.

I generally do not want to have a wrecked car, I do not want my house to burn down, and I sure as heck do not want to be sued in court for loss of another person's property or an injury of another person.

I buy all kinds of insurance -- and so do you.

If you are really wealthy and only want to cover the liability of hurting someone else with your car, then don't buy collision insurance. Or have a very high deductible.

You can afford to self-insure if you have thousands of dollars in the bank.

But life insurance? The irrational arguments about life insurance are many. I listed some in Chapter 7 and will address one here, the "I won't die any time soon" excuse.

Probably true; but if you do die, by accident or serious illness, you no longer have that excuse or any other one.

You will have done the greatest disservice to your loved ones that I have ever witnessed, and I have seen it more than I want to say.

I have seen one man die in Vietnam with lots of life insurance and one man die with only the government GI insurance. The former's wife had a house paid for, his children went on to college, and the goals he had for his family were met through life insurance.

The latter man's wife became a waitress (and there is no dishonor in that work) but she was not able to provide college for his children or keep the house -- not a pretty outcome.

The chart on the next page shows the facts about dying from the 2010 U.S. Census.

Age	All	Male	Female
	Number of American people alive at the stated age by All and by Gender.		
0	100.00	100.00	100.00
25	98.48	98.11	98.88
30	98.01	97.44	98.60
35	97.47	96.72	98.25
40	96.80	95.88	97.75
45	95.83	94.70	96.99
50	94.30	92.82	95.80
55	92.00	90.01	94.02
60	88.77	85.98	91.58
65	84.35	80.66	88.04
70	78.07	73.37	82.76
75	69.30	63.52	75.04
80	57.19	50.41	63.82
85	41.50	34.25	48.34
90	23.62	17.49	29.18
95	9.09	5.67	12.01
100	1.97	0.96	2.76

To use this chart, find your nearest age, for example, male age 30. The number is 97.

Then find the age you want to live to, for example, male age 65. That number is 80. That means 80 of all males born are still alive.

From your current age number, 97, subtract the male age 65 number, 80 (97 - 80 = 17). Seventeen of all thirty year old males will die by age 65.

For a percentage take 17 and divide by 97 and you have 17.5%.

If you are thirty years old today, you have a 17.5% of dying by age 65.

Maybe more relevant is the chance of dying before your children make it out of college. Once again, take a male age 30 and assume he lives to age 50 (92 – 97 = 5). Then divide 5 by 97 equals 5%. A much better outcome.

But when you are part of the 5% it is 100%. And even at age 50 what does that leave a surviving spouse?

We also know that lifestyle issues, such as smoking, obesity, and heredity have a significant influence on these numbers. And of course, Males have the lowest no matter what the parameter.

My question to you is: "Are you willing to take that risk when can turn it into a part of your tax-advantaged portfolio?"

How much and what type should you have

If you meet with a trusted insurance agent he or she will perform a needs analysis by asking you what you currently have for life insurance and assets; and what you want to have for assets "when." ("When" is a euphemism for dying.)

Remember the chart of the Level Universal Life Insurance Policy in Chapter 7? That chart can also be used to project a lifetime of needs versus assets.

Here is the correct strategy.

As you live and contribute to your assets by using pay yourself first, you are building a base upon which to fund your life. As you save for college expenses and your children reach college age, you now have the assets created to pay for college. As a result you no longer have the risk of death preventing you from having the funds to send your children to college.

In a like manner, if you live in the same house you bought when you were thirty, and are now fifty, you no longer have the entire mortgage to pay off. At that point it should be just under half of the original amount.

In other words your lifetime assets are growing and your lifetime liabilities are shrinking.

And so should your life insurance needs. How you manage that is important and a bit complex.

Let us assume that you are just age 30. You are married and have two children, ages 2 and 5. Your salary is $75,000 and your spouse also works and earns $50,000. You have minimal group term insurance.

You determine that to ensure your spouse would be able to raise the children after your death and fund their college savings plan you need to have a lump sum of $750,000 in death benefits. Conversely, if your spouse died you would need life insurance death benefit of $500,000.

As you can see, I have used the rule of ten times salary in this example as it is usually a very good estimate.

Next, how would you structure your life insurance plan? Here is what I would propose.

1. Each of you obtains a $250,000 fifteen year level term policy.

2. Each of you obtains a $250,000 level variable universal life insurance policy.

3. You obtain a $250,000 increasing variable universal life insurance policy.

Regarding premiums they should be as follows:

1. Term will be level and fixed for fifteen years. This will be a budget item. You should not be using your pay yourself first funds for these two policies as you absolutely must have this amount of life insurance for your basic needs should either of you die.

2. Level variable universal life premiums will be based on your pay yourself first cash flow. Begin by paying the minimum required premium into these two policies to ensure that they remain in force for fifteen years. At fifteen years, when the term policies terminate, then add that premium to the payments for these two policies.

3. Increasing variable universal life premium on just you will be the primary policy to fund with as much of your cash flow as you have. Ever dollar over the internal cost of insurance is an invested dollar. (Note: the IRS has limits on how much you can pay into a life insurance policy each year. Check with your agent.)

In all three of the variable policies you will be managing the mutual funds provided by the insurance carriers in the same manner as you manage your Roth IRA accounts and 401(k) if you have one too.

You are using these policies to create tax deferred cash value for use in your future retirement.

WARNING: Remember that you must be healthy to get the best rates for life insurance. Even if you have minor health issues, or if you smoke, you will still need to fund this plan.

By obtaining all of these policies at a young age when you are most certainly going to be in the best health, you are assuring your future life insurance needs.

I have seen the heartbreak of those who have had a heart attack in their forties and suddenly they want life insurance.

I have actually witnessed an older man remain with an employer who offered a large group life insurance plan even though he hated his job. As a result he had to forgo an offer to move to a better job at another company because they had no group life insurance. He had become uninsurable due to health in his late thirties.

Life insurance structured as I have proposed does these three things:

1. Assures that your financial future you have planned for your family will be completed in the event of your untimely death.

2. Is will be able to provide a significant part of your retirement cash portfolio.

3. It will provide you and your family peace of mind. And that's priceless.

One last comment. I counseled a young couple once who had plenty of life insurance and they were proud to say that it would make sure that their children would get to college if one of them died.

I then burst their bubble by asking this question: "How are your children going to get through college if you don't die. Where will that money come from if you both live?"

That's when they realized that it takes both death coverage and life coverage.

Only a small number of children will be sent to college on life insurance death benefits. You can see from the statistics that you most likely will live; therefore, you will need a pile of money someday.

As a result of my comment they vowed to work on a budget and to begin paying themselves first.

I gave them an old copy of the first edition of this book and as I continued to meet with them over the past couple of years their zeal has not failed. They are ardently catching up on the savings and investment end of their lifetime goals by doing two things.

First, they increased their premiums into existing life insurance policies where they could (they had term and universal life).

Second, they opened Roth IRAs and will be able to withdraw the basis for college funds when needed (the children are under age ten so they will clearly meet the five year qualification). That basis will be close to $100K by the time they start college.

They both have 401(k)'s where they can borrow against those accounts too.

There may be some other options in the future, but from my point of view, the most important event was that they recognized their goals and have taken steps to attain them whether they live or die.

STEP FOUR: Own your own home

Owning your own home is an important step after you have been able to do the first three steps for a myriad of reasons.

One of the most important reasons is it is yours. You can paint the walls any color you want, plant flowers you want, and have a pet if you want.

But even more serious you have a stake in the American dream. You have a base to raise your family and enjoy the camaraderie of neighbors.

And, if you are stable in your employment, you will have the time to achieve some long term appreciation in your home.

If your family or your income grows you may choose to move to a larger home. If that occurs, or you are transferred, remember that your first home may be an ideal property to keep and convert to a rental property.

Many a couple (or individual) that I have known in my lifetime began their process to wealth by keeping the first, and sometimes the second property that they lived in so long as they were suitable for being good candidates for long-term rentals. I mentioned this in Chapter 6.

Before the Tax Cuts and Jobs Act of 2017, there were other important aspects of owning your own home through tax advantages.

First, you could deduct the annual property taxes on your income tax return. Beginning in 2018 this is limited to $10,000.

Second, if you have a mortgage, and most of you will, you can deduct the interest paid on that loan on your tax return.

These two considerations are only available to those taxpayers who are able to itemize on Schedule A of Form 1040 (this is technical jargon) and have a total of all their deductions that is greater than the minimum standard deduction.

The standard deduction for 2017 was $6,350 for a single taxpayer and $12,700 for a married couple. Beginning in 2018 this has been raised to $12,000 single and $24,000 married filing jointly.

This has been estimated to eliminate almost half of all middle class taxpayers from itemizing on Schedule A. Now it impacts you can be assessed by doing a comparison with your tax preparer or using an online analysis tool.

As a result of the tax law change effective in 2018 the tax advantages of home ownership have been significantly reduced. But once again, you own a home primarily for the value of being yours.

Third, if the time comes to sell your home, and you have a substantial gain in value, so long as you lived in the home for two of the prior five years you are allowed an exemption of $250,000 for an individual owner; $500,000 for a married couple. (Note: this is the current IRC and may be increased; but I doubt it will ever be terminated.)

This exemption from capital gains tax on the appreciation of your personal residence is a great tax advantage for those who remain in a home for many years and then either move or retire and sell their home.

There are still tax advantages to owning your home, but the principle reason will be that it is yours. Remember that first.

STEP FIVE: Rental real estate

This is the last step because it is the most complex and is usually the most difficult to complete.

I have outlined the tax benefits and some of the issues. And most ardently I recommended that if you do keep your first or second home as rental real estate you have a manager take care of them since most likely you will no longer be living in that city.

For those who believe in rental properties as a major path to wealth, buying properties for the sole purpose of being part of your portfolio requires both skill and work.

I do recommend to those of you who choose to be property owners be very sure about it. You must be able to withstand vacancies, repairs, especially the unexpected when the A/C unit breaks down, etc.

But, if you have all of the other bases covered in this five step plan, then by all means diversify into rental property.

If you live in a growing metro-plex and are able to stay there (no transfers for jobs) then adding rental properties to your portfolio makes great sense. Here's why.

When you retire you want cash income. Yes, you will have 401(k) and Roth IRA funds, as well as cash value in life insurance, but to access those funds depletes their future earning power.

Remember as you withdraw funds from your retirement accounts the balance goes down. At some time they may be depleted.

Conversely, if the mortgage is paid off on rental properties, and the rents have increased over the years, you suddenly have an asset that keeps on paying without depleting the asset's base value. In fact, the value of that asset may continue to increase.

As time goes by rents go up and your income from the properties also goes up. Rental income is sweet.

Just monitor the properties' area, use a manager, and if the area begins to decline consider selling and move your funds to another area or asset account. This can happen. Be cautious.

I will share with you that the best paying properties I ever had were the lowest cost and not in the best neighborhoods. The cap rate was high; but so were the repairs from time to time. Just a word of caution.

Five Steps to Financial Freedom strategy conclusion

I know this may sound trite, but these five steps will serve every level of income, albeit perhaps rental real estate may escape those at lower income levels. But that would be no excuse for not using the first three.

And, if your circumstances change at some point, make it your goal to own your own home.

Remember in Chapter 3 where I stated: "TIME is your friend when you have it; your enemy when you don't!"

Use time as your friend, even if you are fifty years old. You still have twenty years to get there. You can delay taking social security (which I am going to address in the next chapter) and grow a side fund in a Roth IRA.

Yes, these five steps, or one or two of them, can still be used even later in life.

It is your life. Don't throw away your financial future.

Chapter 10: Final thoughts

There are two other considerations that I have not addressed up to this point: the first is Social Security; and the second is small business ownership.

There has been so much said about Social Security over the past fifteen years, in print articles, on the internet, through the grapevine, and politicians taking aim at this program, that very few young adults today have any idea what to think.

Politicians call Social Security the "third rail" of politics yet seem to work more to scare us than to fix the problems that exist. As a result many older adults have a serious concern about Social Security.

The doomsayers tell us it is going broke; the naysayers tell us it won't be there for the young people of today; and the politicians wring their hands after having badly mismanaged the program over the last thirty years.

According to data released by the Social Security Administration and other governmental sources, over half of older Americans rely on Social Security as their main retirement income.

Worse, approximately one-fourth of current retirees over age 65 rely on Social Security benefits for ninety percent of their income. Most of these individuals have been in the lower income groups their entire working lifetime.

Social Security was implemented in 1936. In 2015, fifty-nine million Americans were receiving it: forty million retirees; nine million disabled workers, and ten million survivors.

The actuaries for the Social Security trustees say that if it is not changed, in about 2034 benefits will be cut to 79% of what they are today. Given there will still be a lot of Baby Boomers around I feel pretty sure that something will be changed before then.

In my humble opinion some form of government operated and funded retirement plan will be with us for a very long time. There are just too many people who rely upon it and vote!

I hope so. Although I will be 90 years old when it goes broke in 2034 (laughter included); I intend to still be cashing my check. I am an eternal optimist.

So what do I think the role Social Security benefits should play in your financial plan?

First, should you die after becoming qualified for benefits (a sliding scale for young workers), your spouse can be paid a survivor benefit for each of your children until they are eighteen years old (19 if still a student in K-12).

If your child is disabled there are potential long term benefits (I am not addressing this as there are a lot of rules).

Second, Social Security provides disability benefits to you if qualified (currently requires ten years of work). You may have a disability plan at work; or Social Security may be your only one.

Disability is four times more likely during your working years than death at age 30, three times at age 40, and two times at age 50. That is because death from heart disease has fallen while disability has risen (more people survive the heart attack today).

And disability income protection is expensive so it is rarely purchased other than by high income professionals.

Third, your un-remarried spouse can claim survivor benefits at age 60 (if you have worked at least ten years).

Surviving widow benefits are a complex area and good advice is needed as her income, your income, and reductions for taking any benefits early all have consequences.

Fourth, you and your spouse will be able to eventually retire and draw lifetime retirement benefits. How much is always up to congress, but as I said, I am an eternal optimist.

If only one spouse worked, or both worked, or one spouse made a lot more money, especially if over the maximum income level every year, then your check may be a very nice amount.

For example, I have a cousin who married in college and his wife never worked outside the home. He was a corporate executive and made the maximum every year. He had retired from work at age 64 but waited until his full retirement age at 66 to draw his Social Security benefit making it as high as possible.

By doing so his wife, who was within one month of his age, was able to draw one-half of his amount. That is the spousal benefit if she waits until her normal retirement age.

Then, should my cousin die first (most likely outcome) his wife will then receive his full check as hers. For them Social Security has become a very good supplemental benefit.

Finally, Social Security is a lifetime income that, unlike a 401(k) pension plan which may run out of money.

Social Security has annual cost of living adjustments. It also has survivor and joint income benefits that would have reduced the amount paid by a traditional pension plan or insurance annuity.

When you have paid yourself first, Social Security becomes that extra income you will have when you retire and can spend as you want. For me, it covers my entire housing cost; and upon my death, my wife will continue to have that same income too.

Looking back, when I was ten I thought the day I would be 65 was so far away it was impossible to calculate (congress did move it 66 for me). Now I wonder how it came so fast.

Life is short. Don't waste it.

The second consideration I want to address as another way to achieve future financial freedom is small business ownership.

From the book "The Millionaire Next Door" by Thomas J. Stanley and William D. Danko published in 1996 and based on many years of research by them, I want to share several key factors they pointed out about the individuals who became millionaires with little notice nor fanfare. Here are some of their key findings:

- They did not inherit wealth. About four out of five of them were first generation rich having little given them by their parents.
- The individuals studied could best be described as "tightwads." They were frugal and lived well below their incomes. They drove older cars and did not spend for keeping up with the Jones things (remember that I listed that as one of the obstacles to your success in Chapter 3). I still drive a beautiful 2004 Cadillac Deville DTS.
- Nearly all had major stock holdings and rarely traded. They had a long-term investment philosophy and simply let their holdings ride. No day traders here.
- Half of them owned their own business. This was a major factor.

It is this last point, small business ownership, which I wish to expand upon as I have not previously addressed it.

This book is aimed at the average employed individual who will spend his or her lifetime working for a company, or in a career profession.

I totally concur that a way to wealth is through owning a small business. I have met many who have done so.

For example, I met a man who bought a McDonald's franchise when he was thirty-five. Although he had a good job he wanted to be his own boss. He used all of his savings and borrowed the rest to get started. He worked long hours every day and rarely took time away from the business.

Over time, thirty years later when I met him, he owned six McDonald's and was very wealthy.

Business owners tend to plow all of their excess income back into their business; thus, paying yourself first occurs every day of their working lives by growing and expanding their business.

I have also known two other individuals who made it big by owning Sonic drive-ins, and another who created his own idea of a good taco stand. He now has three in the area I lived in Dallas.

There are thousands of such individuals and in all types of trades and professions. As another example, when you see a Pink Cadillac with a Mary Kay logo on the back window you are seeing a woman who plied her way through hundreds of cosmetic parties over many years and succeeded.

Conversely, I also know many who failed in the pursuit of their dream to be their own boss. Not every venture works; not every person can handle the task. And some choose not to pay the price of so much time away from their family.

The man who first introduced me to sales in Hawaii made his fortune in Amway in Japan (yes they buy soap there too); and then lost a great deal of it in the securities firm he created in Hawaii after that.

It didn't help him, or me, that the 1986 tax code changes (recall my outline of the history of the income tax in Part 3) enacted at that time ended the tax benefits for the products he was selling.

I was successful in the military (I was promoted right along the way) but I wanted more. I retired right at twenty years and went into sales where I met a man who became my partner.

Together, he and I and some very good employees created a small company offering a specialty consulting service. We grew to twenty-five employees and reached clients in twenty-six states. Five years later we sold it to a larger consulting company.

Following that sale, unfortunately, I learned the old adage about how to make a small fortune in the aviation business is to start with a large fortune. It is true.

I had joined with an individual in another state who had contracts to import former Eastern Bloc jet trainers and warbirds. I bought and remodeled a large hangar at a north Texas airport and began hiring employees. Our plan was to sell these trainers and warbirds to wealthy doctors and other pilots and provide the required FAA qualification and insurance carrier's annual training.

I put all of the money from selling my share of the consulting company into this new aviation company and opened the doors to my very large renovated hangar on April 1st, 2001.

On September 11th, 2001, my dream was shattered. Our "fighter" planes were considered high threats to national security and were grounded for an extended period of time.

The FAA then imposed new maintenance and flight restrictions on these aircraft and our contracts in Poland and Czechoslovakia were cancelled. The value of those jets plunged. My business was over, just like that.

I personally owned two jet trainers and eventually I sold my hangar and those two jets for twenty percent of what I paid for them; and went limping back to work as a consultant.

I share this because one has to be able to stand the risk of being in business as well as be able to personally bounce back if it fails.

I did. I have always been a great salesman and optimist and that will not change. Not for 9-11 or anything else.

<u>Hard facts</u>

Here is some hard data to consider if you think starting your own business is for you.

The U.S. Bureau of Labor Statistics reports that about half of all employer establishments survive at least five years and a third survive ten years or more.

Other sources have some other data based on size of the startup and product. They say that up to one-third fail in the first year, especially very small mom and pop companies, and half by four years.

The point is starting your own business is risky; but the reward can be great. If that is your dream go for it. Remember Colonel Sanders failed many times before he got it right in his '60's!

And if not for Thomas Edison, without trying an estimated 10,000 times to create the electric light bulb, I might be writing this by a gas light, which, by the way, was one of the companies that Colonel Sanders failed in when rural electrification came to Kentucky!

We live in America where anyone can reach his or her dream. But if it is not to be, then you need the time and the spirit to pick yourself up and try again; and perhaps again.

Thank god I did.

"Success is not final; failure is not fatal; it is the courage to continue that counts."

- Winston S. Churchill (1874 - 1965)

Conclusion
"Pay Yourself First works"

I could stop right now with the above statement.

If you have read this entire book and have the desire to obtain wealth by the time you retire and put your children through college, then I have laid out a plan that works.

But recall the discussion of poverty consciousness in Chapter 2 and some obstacles to success in Chapter 3.

If you become faint of heart please re-read those two chapters.

You may find it hard to stay the course of paying yourself first. Giving up satisfaction today for a benefit tomorrow is hard to do. I know that.

At the seminars I did for years I would tell the attendees that most people spend more time planning one vacation than they do planning their financial life.

The heads in the audience would nod approval; then many left with no intent of doing anything.

But those that stayed, and the majority did, became far wealthier by working with my consulting company. And many would say when we had completed our work with them: "Why doesn't everyone do this?"

"Why doesn't everyone do this?"

Take a look again at the page to your left. Winston Churchill's quote says it all.

About the author

Lynn O. High is a retired career military officer and an experienced financial consultant, lecturer and author.

To quote excerpts from the first edition of this book, "The experiences he writes about have been gained over the years from the school of hard knocks. Having tried just about every "get rich quick" scheme there is, he has learned three secrets about the art of investing that he willingly shares in this book."

Continuing, "If you think about it, what better way for you to profit than by avoiding his mistakes and use his successes."

Mr. High holds a bachelor's degree in economics and a master's degree in business administration. He served twenty years in the U.S. Air Force during which time he attended the Armed Forces Staff College and the Air War College.

Upon being commissioned a second lieutenant he entered pilot training graduating first in his class. He had two combat tours in the Vietnam War as a fighter pilot flying the F-100 and the F-4.

For his combat service and heroism he was awarded three Silver Stars, four Distinguished Flying Crosses, the Purple Heart, and thirty-eight Air Medals.

Following retirement from the air force he joined a marketing firm that sold special products to community banks. Eventually, with a partner, they formed a national consulting firm offering seminars through securities companies and trade associations.

His professional work included estate planning for high net worth individuals as well as financial counseling for the general public. After he retired in 2010 he became a tax professional with a national company and is an enrolled agent with the IRS.

He is the author of several books available today and during his air force career was a prolific writer in aircraft journals and service magazines.

His first book was the first edition of this book which he self-published and sold through direct marketing and seminar presentations. He also wrote "The Ten Commandments of Wealth" and sold it through securities companies.

In 2014 he wrote an autobiography of this first seven years in the air force focusing on his two years in combat. It was published in 2015 and is available through major book retailers.

In 2016 he wrote another autobiography about his sales careers with an emphasis on how he developed the sales skills to close multi-million dollar sales. He tells how he used humor as well as sound presentations skills to be a four time national sales leader during fifteen years.

Now you have the benefit of over forty-five years of his investing experience and can implement the Five Steps to Financial Freedom strategy presented in this book.

Enjoy it, follow it, and prosper.

(List of books on next page.)

Books written by Lynn O. High

The following books have been published by the author:

Pay Yourself First, 1984, revised 1985, 2017 and 2018

The Ten Commandments of Wealth, 1985, revised 2017

Born to be a Warrior, 2015 (Page Publishing, New York)

Whisky Women and War, 2017

Combat Jet Pilot, 2017

All of these books are available on Amazon and Kindle (except Born to be a Warrior) also available at retail book stores).

The author has a website to learn more about each book at:
www.lynnhighbooks.com